Spirituality and the Relational in a Trilogy.

Meeting Emma
The Primacy of Love
The Language of Love.

Three modern stories about the love of God and people. It offers insights on many topics and freshens up the Christian faith. Some ideas are new, others simply important. Do care to be different - read and reflect. Theology can be fun!

Each book is an independent read.

The Primacy of Love

Theological Conversations
in the Simpson Desert

Michael J Spyker

AgapeDeum

Published in Adelaide, Australia by AgapeDeum
Contact: agapedeum.com

ISBN 978-0-6486957-4-5

This edition published in 2020

Publication assistance by Immortalise
Cover design: Ben Morton

.

TABLE OF CONTENT

PART ONE

PART TWO

PART ONE

1

The primacy of love and a relational universe

THE SKY IS BLACK and wide with uncountable stars twinkling brightly. It is a typical Australian outback night sky. Everything is quiet, apart from the soft movement of flames in the open fire. Jake prods it a little with a stick and throws on another log. There is a chill in the air which the fire keeps at bay if you sit close. Jake is my godson in his early twenties, the only son of my best friend, who died some years ago. His name is Jacob actually, but as a child when first speaking that out it sounded like Jake. Soon, it became Jakey as an affectionate calling and now it is Jake. He likes it better than Jacob and I must admit: so do I.

Just before dark we cooked our dinner in the open fire using a long-handled cast iron skillet. The blackened kettle that boils our water for coffee lies discarded to one side. It is amazing how hot a fire gets and the speed at which the water boils. With dinner the trick is not to burn the food, use a bit of oil, keep stirring and if needed place the skillet at a less hot spot. These are easy skills and it makes bush cooking rather attractive. We have wiped our plates with paper towels after dinner with the last ones being wetted a little from the water container. That paper has long disintegrated in the flames. Water is scarce in the desert; you will only have what you bring along and soon learn to become effective in cleaning things, and yourself as well, using as little as possible.

A few days ago we started our journey on bitumen and later dirt roads. Last night we camped at Dalhousie Springs. It features a large pond with water that remains warm regardless of the outside temperatures that, at times, can be below zero. Jake and I had taken a dip and floated about. The water was too warm for a real swim. Dalhousie is a favourite place for families with children, if you can make it that far over rough roads and tracks. Rubber tire tubes and spaghetti floaters await those in need of them at the edge of the spring. Since Dalhousie, Jake and I have followed the French Line, a track of red sand, miles of it. There are sand hills to get over, about 1000 of them. We are in the Simpson Desert, the largest parallel sand hills desert in the world at the centre of Australia. Late this afternoon we pulled up at a flat open space just off the track. It would be our campsite for the night featuring some bushes in the stark landscape. I heard a noise a few minutes ago and shone my LED torch deep into the dark. Two yellow eyes glistened at a distance. Not quite as alone as we thought. There would be a dingo or two moving about.

Jake has become reflective. It is what the desert does to you and an open fire also. Life slows down when bush camping. The manner in which he stares into the flames reminds me of his father; the similarity in looks and the stillness around his person. Liam could be like that, just suddenly at times, particularly when a thought came to mind that he considered important and which needed attention. His untimely death was a shattering blow. Jake was 16 years of age then.

'Another beer?'

Our camping has a few mods and cons including a fridge/freezer run from a second deep cycle battery in the back of a pickup which in Australia is called a "ute", short for utility. This car, with a two seats cabin and a large one-ton loading tray that is covered with a high canopy, has served me well over the years. The car's diesel engine and designated four-wheel drive gearbox are powerful. Apart from a flat tire by cutting the side of it on a rock it has never let me down.

Jake nods his head to the question of beer and keeps on staring. When I toss him a coldy, he catches it with the ease of the good cricketer he is. There are two empty cans next to the fire already. Two a day each is our ration unless we would decide to run out of beer before the end of the trip. The closest pub is at Birdsville, many miles away and our destination.

'The power of purification,' I say, also looking into the flames. The fire has burned long enough for the larger bits of wood to be orangey red-hot all through.

'Combustion.' Always Jake likes to be accurate when describing phenomena.

'I was referring to John of the Cross.'

He gives me a quick look with a sideways turn of the head. 'I should have guessed,' he says, without any sense of scorn. Jake knows of my interest in all things spiritual and neither agrees nor rejects it. His main interest is mathematics and philosophy and in keeping an open mind. He has graduated in his first degree and continues studying. 'What about John of the Cross?' he asks, always ready to gather information that might be of interest.

'John considered the sight of logs completely taken by fire and glowing bright red a symbol of the purification powers of God,' I explain. 'That's mostly meaningful for saints.'

'Counts me out,' Jake observes. This statement is simply spoken and halts the conversation.

I enjoy Jake's presence for I like young people. I know

him to be a person who will not easily become angry with his circumstances, however bad it may get at times. He is sensitive, but without smouldering emotionally when hurt. Not helpful, he once explained. It only messes me up.

As I look up at the sky, the immensity of it all and the stars so much clearer than you will ever see in the city, I cannot help but say: 'And it is all held together in love.' This comment shakes Jake out of his reverie and he looks at me. I had not intended that, know what he is thinking, and chide myself.

'That's what my father used to say – many times.'

'Yes, I know,' I confess. It made me say it.

'He told me, he would explain in detail when I would be older.' Jake is back at staring into the fire, but with his stillness gone and a slight tightening of the jaws.

'Yeah.' Certainly, in time Liam would have told Jake all about his theories.

Both of us fall silent thinking about the same person.

'You know of his thoughts more that anyone,' Jake suggests, eventually.

I admit that I do and become aware of my young friend's deep pain from a loss that will not be restored. Beside me sits a son who was promised so, but never would be taught by his father. It is sad.

'Will you tell me about them, those thoughts,' Jake

asks a minute later.

This request I sense has been a while in coming. Perhaps some months ago in Adelaide Jake might have agreed to our bush bash for this very reason. He would never tell me and it completely doesn't matter. How can I not introduce him to the insightful ideas of his father; ideas that have so much enriched my life.

Whenever he was amongst a group of people, you could always find Liam talking to those who stood mostly alone. That is how we met, now many years ago. He could talk to anyone and was completely non-judgmental. Except when someone annoyed him and that could happen. Then he would mutter something to get it off his chest but not harbour any grudges. Talking to people is not that hard, he once explained. You simply ask some questions and make sure you are really interested. That is exactly what had happened to me after the worship service in a church I visited for the first time. Being a rather private person, I kept my answers friendly, but short. Liam seemed not to notice. He had the gregarious nature of someone who likes company. People never were a number in the pack to him. He was attractive to be with.

It was immediately obvious that this attraction extended to the opposite sex, though Liam never gave any indication that he was aware of it. He had not a predatory bone in his body. When eventually he married, it was because he well and truly fell in love with Sandy, and because she suggested they should become engaged. Liam readily agreed, was slow in planning the wedding, and they were always happy together. But, that was years later.

When I first met him he was a high school teacher not long out of college with a degree in economics. Why economics, I once asked. Nothing like you Baz and the precise science of structural engineering, he had said. Economics tries to be quite precise in its theories like mathematics, but in reality it remains unpredictable in outcomes for it involves the behaviour of people. People are fascinating. So, it's not a closed shop. That appeals to me. The mind must be allowed to roam, he would say.

Liam remained single for a long time. He decided after two years of teaching to save part of his salary for another three and then commence a study in theology. During these studies he would supplement his money with what he made from tutoring a few graduand high school students. Over time he became a fine New Testament theologian. The only drawback was that theology can be picky with views competing aggressively with each other. That totally annoyed Liam. His thinking, though very disciplined, was too broad and original for the arguing common in theological circles. He could acknowledge the merits of good ideas and accept some argumentation, but not when it became scrappy. He felt that truth about God is expansive and yet fundamentally not overly complicated. The Gospel is not that difficult to understand, he would insist. You must take the right perspective and make sure not to become bogged down in the detail. How can God be better understood by a deconstruction of the idea of God into a myriad of small bits of reasoning? He had his preferred theologians, but never became a follower of one in particular. His students loved him for it. He suggested a measure of simplicity, but reflected on the idea of God deeply and in detail all the same.

Over time Liam discovered a key to understanding the Gospel and developed it consistently. The path was staring me in the face for years, he would say. You have to begin with love. It is love where everything begins and ends. Not wishy-washy love, but the love of God. The universe only exists because of love and everything that happens in the end is love related. Start with love and it all makes sense, eventually. His ideas about love extended well beyond the general notion of what love is about.

We discussed this premise and its development regularly over the years. New perspectives always made Liam happy and ever more in awe of his Lord. Why didn't I see that before? he would wonder. My own increasing knowledge about spirituality was of some help, as were my analytical tendencies. Baz, you bring new perspectives and your precise engineering brain picks out the structural flaws in my ideas without fail. That was an overstatement, if ever I heard one.

In a way we grew into full manhood together, Liam and I, sort of from our first meeting. I married Liv well before Liam ever had met Sandy. My marriage made no difference to our lasting friendship. Liv understood how important he was to me. Nice, he once said, your names are meant for each other: Bastian and Olivia. You are the bastion and she is the oil that keeps everything running smoothly. It was a pertinent observation. Now Liam is no more and I am sitting with his only son around a fire in the middle of nowhere. Two men with a loss, though Jake is carrying by far the greater.

'He was going to write a book,' Jake says.

'Yes, I know.'

'Why don't you write it?'

I could never do that. Most of what Liam's book would be about I can readily guess, but a theologian I'm not. I could not possibly do Liam's work justice. Also, few people would read such a book, I being not known in theological circles. I tell Jake that.

'So his ideas will be lost,' Jake concludes.

'Many good ideas are, Jake. Even the ideas that make it, only tend to shine for a short season and then the world moves on.' Our world is one of too much information and only what can be readily digested may find some traction.

Jake nods almost imperceptibly, picks up a stick and prods the fire. I can sense his mind fighting with his sadness. Then he looks at me straight and concludes: 'But you will tell me?'

There is a slight challenge in his voice.

'Yes. I will, if you like.'

'So that I can write a book. If, I want to.'

No doubt one day Jake will be able to write a book on a matter that interests him. Presently, he is sticking up for his father and the futility of many years of thoughtful thinking now sadly lost forever. A kind of desperate act. Touched by this, I gaze into the fire for a while once more. The flames are lively making wonderful patterns of blue, yellow and red while jumping in and out of existence.

'I will tell enough for you to well understand your dad's views on life,' is my response. 'If you make it your own, you may eventually write a book that could include it. Time will tell. Perhaps you will believe like Liam did. Perhaps, you won't.'

'Okay' Jake can see the wisdom in that. 'And thanks, Baz. Dad said that without you, he wouldn't have got as far. '

A glimpse of Liam's smiling face glides through my mind. Jake's comment doesn't really me. Nice to know, but quite incorrect.

He sips his beer. 'When do we start?'

Youth is always in a hurry. But then patience is not one of my virtues either. 'Might as well begin now,' I suggest. 'It will take a few campfires to tell.'

Jake relaxes. Like Liam, he is a sponge and a filter, who loves being soaked in information.

'Liam asked the very fundamental question that if God *is* Love,[1] may it then be that love has primacy in all that exists,' I begin. 'After all, God will not initiate a creation that misaligns with God's own nature.'

Jake listens attentively.

'Furthermore,' I continue, 'Scripture instructs that creation holds together in Christ, the Son of God.[2] Christ is the source of all existential reality.' I give it a moment for those two statements to sink in.

'The source?' Jake queries.

'Yes. Creation originates in Christ, who is love. With Christ I mean the eternal Son of God, not his physical appearance while he walked in Israel.'

'So, without the Son of God there would be no creation,' Jake decides. 'And the foundation of creation is love. Looking at our suffering world, that's hard to believe – about love.'

'True. What love involves must be defined to account for that problem. We shall discuss that later.'

Jake nods his acceptance.

'An important point about love is that by nature it is relational. Or rather, relation is a dynamic that derives from love, you might say.'

'Love is the source of relationality,' Jake rephrases my statement.

'Yes. And with everything existing in love, which itself is relational, it means that in essence everything is relational.' This idea is central in Liam's theology.

'So, we live in a relational universe,' Jake observes.

I ask him whether he has heard that phrase from his father. He admits this to be so.

'All originates from love and is relational, that is the premise. Liam concluded that creation is in a constant state of divine nurture, the nurture of love.'

'What about sin?' Jake wonders.

'Sin is also relational, but it's not primary. The power of sin is undeniable, but it will be temporary.'

Jake smiles contentedly. He perceives a number of philosophical discussions to be ahead. His eyes have brightened up.

'For Liam, ideas were most useful if they could find a practical application,' I continue, 'or at least they must assist in helping to explain our reality.'

I tell Jake about panentheism, the technical term for the notion that God is in everything, which does not make everything God. Essentially, God remains beyond our existential reality. Jake handles that idea with ease. Liam concluded, that if God's love resides in everything and is relational, then possibly the relational dynamics that are primary in bringing bring wellbeing to our world might be decided on. They would align with the dynamics of love. Liam derived insights on this from a study of the Trinity and presented it in a Trinitarian Relational Model. In the model he contrasted the dynamics of love with those of sin. I promise Jake a copy of it once back in Adelaide and tell him that Liam's research was based on various sources. It involved a spectrum of questions on love, relating, the universe and good living. Scripture and theology were to be the main guide, but he also used philosophy and psychology. If Jake wants all that information, it will become quite a journey of discovery.

Of course, Jake desires the full story. But the hour is getting late and the night rather cold. It is time for our sleeping bags.

2

Eternal and universal love; derivatives of love and sin

I AM SWINGING THE STEERING WHEEL heavily. In the Simpson Desert the track over the top of a sand dune when travelling west to east usually veers to the right. All the hills run north to south. The prevailing wind in the desert is west and it creates a kind of sand cushion on the lee side of the crest. For a moment you will slide downhill trying to see where exactly the track leads. This descent can be steep and throw the car sideways into bushes, or it may be gentle. Your responses must be quick and rolling a car is possible. The bonnet sticks up into the air when I reach the summit and only by looking along the side of the bonnet can I detect how serious a turn needs to be taken. Often even that view is hidden and so it is now. I crest over the sand hill blindly for a second or two. A sand flag has been fitted to the bull-bar, just a tall flexible pole with a bright triangular flag up top. It will warn travellers coming up the other side of the dune of our presence before they see our vehicle; just in time to put on the brakes if necessary. These dunes can be a tricky business, but the driving is exciting. Once over, a flat stretch beckons with the next hill on the horizon. It seems never ending. Today I will do the driving. Tomorrow Jake can have a go.

This morning when packing up camp footprints were found right around our tent very close in. The dingo I spotted last night would have been sniffing about. The rule is never to leave anything in the open that might be of interest to these wild dogs and could be dragged away. The fire was still smouldering at sunrise and we brought it back to life. Failing that, I could have used the gas bottle with a cooking ring that travels roped down in the tray of the car. I prefer the open fire. Breakfast always includes filling up the thermos.

On a trip that takes many days talk can be sporadic. Few words are spoken, between people who are happy to dwell with their own thoughts. Jake and I converse little apart from comments on the environment. I told Jake over breakfast that I have no idea how long it will take to relate all of Liam's ideas. We considered suitable times and have decided to make lunch possibly an hour. We can talk then. Our discussions will continue every evening around the fire. It will be a lot of talking, but

Jake insisted that he doesn't mind. He prefers it complete at the end of our holiday and so do I. We will not extend our talks into driving times. That possibly crossing the desert may take longer due to our planned conversations is not a problem. The speed of travel depends on the weather anyway. Going bush always includes extra provision for those unforeseen circumstances. Rain might delay the journey or demand a detour. Presently, the days are fine and no bad weather is expected. We are making good progress.

I reflect on my interest in spirituality. It began with a few books that gave a different perspective on what I under-stood the interaction with God to be. From reading these books I learned about my natural tendency towards contemplation. One thing led to another. I remember a period, for about a month, that I can only explain as experiencing the dark night of the soul. Fortunately, I had read a good description of this experience and was able to last through the dryness and sense of depression without too much concern. There would be an end to it, I was told. Just ride the wave in the meantime. Do not fight it, nor question and worry yourself unnecessarily. God will be at work. The desert we are driving through reminds of it. It is dry, wild and unending, but strangely beautiful with tuffs of Spinifex grass, dark slow growing bushes and in places a low tree.

By nature I am attracted to that. It reminds of the Desert Fathers and Mothers in regions of Egypt and their quest to get closer to God.

One aspect of Liam's search in life was an increasing awareness of its potential spiritual dynamics. He never was a merely technical theologian. Theology without faith and deep reflection, being open to new insights, is like building a house that just stands there, immovably and lifeless. It is designed not to move, not to change easily. Renovations are possible, but slow in coming, and then the rigidity returns. Liam found that theological thought patterns could be overly inflexible, like a game of chess. Everything is predetermined by the rules and board you play on. Any rule change means a major upheaval. He was not so silly to disregard scholarship. However, he allowed for the possibilities of intuition, and creativity – the what-if? Unsurprisingly, he valued metaphysics.

His thoughts were motivated by a deep love for the Lord. His interest in a theology of love resulted from that. Once, he told of an experience that completely surprised and overwhelmed him. Just for a brief moment, sitting in a chair in reflective prayer, the veil over the full reality of God's love was slightly lifted. He was confronted with a vision, or perception rather, that reached beyond the confines of our created world. It came suddenly and passed quickly leaving him completely stumped, as he put it. I sat a long time afterwards quietly in that chair, he said, and what came to my understanding is way beyond the usual. I can't even begin to describe it. God's love is an immeasurably high multiplication of what a person would consider love to be at its most significant. You got to believe me, Baz.

Liam now lives in that love permanently.

'You know what Carl Jung said about love?' I ask Jake at lunch. We had pulled up under a small tree with the sun blazing up above, the desert bright. High trees are non-existent at the centre of this desert due to lack of water. 'He admitted to have again and again been faced with its mystery and never been able to explain what it is.[3] Love is not easily defined and how we usually look at it does no justice at all to its full meaning. It escapes ready qualification.'

'But we all want it,' Jake responds.

'Very much so. Though the way in which we use the word when describing our feelings can be confusing. Actually, love is much more than a feeling.'

'That's your point, isn't it?'

'Yes. But staying with the feeling side for a moment, what is called love can in fact be quite the opposite.'

'Like the boy who loves the girl, but just seeks to

satisfy himself?' Jake is quick off the mark.

'Yes, our use of the word is often not that precise in representing what love really is about.'

I bite into a cracker with fish spread on top. My food supplies always include a good number of small tins with flavoured tuna. The fish stays fresh whatever the weather.

'Liam took the love concept back to its beginning,' I continue. 'He decided that it was divine. Then, he differentiated between the love found in God and that found in creation. The love found in God he classified as *eternal* and the one in creation as *universal* love.[4] It is an important distinction in his theology. For him the word love had significance well beyond the emotional. It is a fundamental force from which everything originates. Human experience, our existential being, finds its origin in *universal* love, Liam decided. Against *eternal* love, which is divine and thus beyond the existential. I will explain that in detail later on.'

I give it a moment for this information to become absorbed. Jake pours the last dregs of his coffee into the sand.

'Another word central to Liam's ideas is the word good. When God created everything, it was declared to be very good.[5] The word good here refers not merely to what we would call excellent, but to paraphrase the meaning: creation represented ultimate goodness. Liam reasoned that God would not have created unless in accordance with God's own nature. If God is love, and creation is declared good, it follows that good is a derivative, an outflow, of God's love.'

'Good is a derivative of *universal* love,' Jake suggests.

'If you mean the existential good, the good in our world, then yes,' I agree. 'However, God is good, which means that goodness is divine and thus eternal and an expression of God's nature.'

'So the good is a derivative of eternal *and* universal love.' Jake nods his acceptance of that idea.

'Not really, for in God there are no derivatives. Only in that which results from God's creative acts.

Jake nods while thinking through this.

'Scripture tells us that creation fell and that sin entered the world. The opposite of good arrived in the form of evil. From that moment on people have had the knowledge of good *and* evil. Sin, of course, is not divine. It has a universal quality, finds its reality in creation. The forces of good and evil are central to how creation, both the transcendent and earthly realms, functions.'

I explain to Jake that the Fall has not been able to sever the ties between love and the good and never will. Sin merely can restrict the existential effectiveness of love and what is good, and it does so enormously. When the good finds expression in our world, its origin still reaches back into the love of God.

Jake mulls this over and revisits the point. 'So good is an outflow of love, God's love actually, and evil is an outflow of sin.'

'Yes. You could call love and sin primary forces that manifest to us as good and evil. Love can be experienced. As people we readily accept that. The influences of sin are also experienced though often not recognised as such. Grief and hurt, for instance, qualify as emotions due to the power of sin in our world, though neither grief nor hurt are sinful as such. Simply, we tend to connect sin more readily to the manifestations of evil or immorality.'

For now, this explanation will suffice. We will continue tonight. I question Jake how familiar he is with theology. Not much, he admits. But you have ideas about God, I press on. Of course he does. As expected those are rather undefined, which a few questions reveal. Though Jake has gone to Sunday school and for a while belonged to a church youth group, his knowledge about God is limited. Our discussions should be fun. Clearly Jake is interested. He has no real idea about Liam's creative intelligence and looks forward to finding out more about his dad. I tell him we shall revisit all the points again and more deeply. I get up and fold my chair. The sun is bright and much lower in the sky than at the height of summer. When the desert is closed to traffic due to extreme heat. A few more miles of red sand are ahead, one hill after another.

3

Common perceptions of love – love as care and mystical love

LIAM'S PRIDE AND JOY was a 1969 MGB GT sports-car, bright red with shiny wire wheels. He exulted in its distinctive Pininfarina lines of Ferrari pedigree and also in the sound of the engine. It is a sound you can recognise immediately if you are familiar with classic cars. Never have I seen the car dirty at the start of a ride. That MG offered a way in which Liam could relax, just polishing it and making one or two improvements. He spent quite a bit of money once having the gearbox replaced with one that had overdrive. When at speed the engine settled into the low growl that this allows for, you could just feel him being content. It was, as if he settled deeper into his seat never to be moved again. Once, he convinced Sandy that taking the car to the snow fields far away at Mount Buller in Victoria, about 600 miles from Adelaide, was feasible. After all, the MG had an English pedigree and that meant that snow should not bother it. It turned out a wonderful trip by all accounts. I wonder what their friends, who had invited them to a chalet at the bottom of the mountain near Mansfield, thought of it. They must have smiled in the recognition that Liam had a knack at being fun and a little larger than life. When he was inspired, he was most pleasant to be with. That could be because of the MG, or theological ideas, or just feeling good for no reason. His eyes would light up like beacons and talk would come easily. There were different sort of days as well. Liam was a complex person.

We were driving along to McLaren Vale, a famous wine region just south of Adelaide, in the MG, naturally. I must admit that I shared his enjoyment. The car was great fun. Liam recounted with a grin that once when he was parked at a plant nursery a young boy had shouted out to his father, look what a small car, dad. By modern standards it was small, which became most apparent with a truck on its tail. So lovely and uncomplicated, Liam would say. You can feel every bit of this car at work. It was true enough. It was a joy motoring along in the little sports car. I drove it a few times myself. In fact, the car is now mine. Sandy persuaded me to buy it. He would have wanted you to have it Baz, she said. The price she accepted was far too low, but I understood why and didn't argue. Liv had no objections. We took the MG to Port Lincoln once, almost as far from Adelaide as Mount Buller, but travelling west instead of east. I had expected that driving a car that once belonged to Liam might give me mixed emotions. It did at first, but not anymore. It now holds fine memories of a fine friend.

At McLaren Vale we settled for lunch at the Tapestry winery. It has a wide open deck in front that allows for far-away views over a landscape full of vines and hills in the distance. These hills are the most southern end of the Flinders Ranges which run north past Adelaide and on for hundreds of miles to offer some of the most spectacular, and most ancient, mountain scenery in Australia at its most northern section. It was autumn amongst the vines. The red and orange colouring of leaves everywhere shone magnificently in the sun. We ordered a plate of antipasto presenting cheese, cold meats and my favourite, pickled octopus. Locally grown kalamata olives were included and olive oils with bread and ground nuts for a dip. A Tapestry Shiraz completed our culinary enjoyment.

'I want to talk about love,' Liam said. 'Did you bring the stuff?'

That stuff involved some pages about the mystical experiences of saints. I confirmed that I had.

'English uses the word love in all kinds of ways,

you know, but it invariably involves a feeling component,' Liam commented.

He proceeded in rattling off some examples between bites of cheese and crackers. The statement, I'd love to go to the ballgame, speaks of desire. When it is said of someone that she loves to play ball, it expresses the enjoyment that person finds in doing so. He surely loves himself, is often a comment on self-appreciation, perhaps excessively. Tears at a funeral reveal love as an emotional attachment, while falling in love refers to an eruption of feelings that are hard to explain. In these few examples love is described as feeling of desire, one of enjoyment and one of appreciation. It is used in referring to an undercurrent of relational belonging and to an explosion of powerful sensations, which mostly are not rational.

I decided just to listen. When Liam was on a roll, that would always be best.

He took a breather, sipped some wine and twirled it around in his glass. His eyes scanned the horizon and his mind the spectrum of love as a word. After a while he appeared to speak to the hills far away. There is being in love and staying in love, he said. Every situation is different, but love always involves the affirmation of the person, activity or situation at which it is directed. Love is the most positive word in the human language. It is what everyone is looking for when given half a chance.

'Do you ever wonder why this is so?' he asked.

It was not a question posed to me for the first time. Liam knew what I would say. 'God has ordained for creation to find its origin in divine love. That love is an active force in our universe, one that attracts us,' I dutifully responded.

'Active and attractive, it is both that. I knew you'd get it right, Baz,' he said with a smile. 'It is also affective, and that seems to be the quality that defines love in the general use of the word. This is far too limiting though. There is much more to love than merely affection.'

'Yes,' I agreed, to help the conversation along.

'The key word about love is care. No care, no love. But how about caring without affectionate emotions, is that still an expression of love? Many people would say it is not, but they are wrong.'

To Liam this was an important point. He continued to explain about the Bible and how love is seen differently there. A person may indeed care with noticeable affection and that will be caring in love. Or, the care may be supported by a sense of relational belonging, in which love may be found as an undercurrent of affections that are mostly subconscious rather than noticeably felt. It can be classified as caring in love. And then, there is the care that simply seeks to do good. There are no affective emotions involved. Interestingly, it is this kind of care for which the word love is often used in Scripture. An example of it is the great commandment: "You must love the Lord your God with all your heart, your soul, your mind and your strength and your neighbour as yourself."[6]

'Is this instruction mostly referring to love as an emotion or love as an intention,' Liam questioned.

'It refers mostly to the second,' I suggested.

'Yes. If positive emotions become associated then so much the better, but it's not essential. You cannot be expected to experience the vibes of love towards every person you encounter. It would be quite unrealistic.'

'True.'

'Jesus even encouraged us to love our enemies,' Liam continued. 'That will hardly involve positive emotions. In Scripture the Greek word for this kind of love is *agape*. It means, always seeking the best for a person, no matter what is done to you.'

I reflected that love as caring is not a new idea. Even so, the simple instruction to love your neighbour as yourself confuses Christians. They don't feel love for their neighbour quite as they think they should. They may also not feel love for God, really. Not in the sense of what love means in the common use of the word. What they fail to understand sufficiently is that the nature of love as encouraged in the Bible is not finally determined by feelings, but by actions. Love without positive action cannot be real love. Most people would agree with that. However, that just doing good without much or any affection is still an expression of love, is less understood. Liam held to the notion that the origin of love predates creation, is primary to it, and 'the good' is a first derivative of love. All 'good things' lead back to a God, who is love, he would say. If so, then even if I don't *feel love* I can at least still *do love* by doing good. God will be pleased and I fulfil my Christian duties.

'Love is a positive action,' Liam continued his exposition. 'An attitude. When Apostle John declared that the love of God is keeping his commandments,[7] there is no reference to feelings in the context in which this advice is found in his letter. It is a matter of: this is what you must do! If you don't, it brings your understanding of God into question. "He who does not love does not know God; for God is love,"[8] Liam quoted from memory.

'If God asks something as important as love of every person, it should be possible for anyone to be successful in it, at least to some extent,' I suggested.

'Of course it is. The ability to care belongs to us all; caring for everything, where possible. Feeding the cat, pruning a tree for quality fruit, helping the neighbour in a task, it fits the idea of love. Even when what is achieved seems quite ordinary, if it is an act of caring, it means doing things God's way.

'And now, after John, you're going to talk about Paul,' I remarked.

Liam grinned. 'You know me too well, Baz. Of course, I will talk about Paul. John and Paul, they are my heroes: the spiritual disciple of love and the incredible theologian. Without Paul we would have no idea of what the Gospel is about.'

'First Corinthian chapter 13, then,' I said and poured myself some more wine. Liam placed his hand over his glass indicating abstinence. He was our MG driver.

'Sure. If you ignore the religious context of Paul's explanation of love, it applies to every person equally. Whoever I may be, if I have not love, I am but like a cracked bell. No matter how powerful, rich or famous you are, without the act of love and caring always being an aim in your life, you are just a shell of a person. That counts for anyone, not just Christians,' Liam stated with some force and continued to elaborate that according to Paul love must be patient and kind, not jealous or boastful. It does not insist on its own way and is not irritable or resentful. It rejoices in what is right, bears and endures all things. Love is everlasting. Liam knew we were both well aware of those words by Paul, but he just took pleasure in speaking them out.

'Everlasting means that when this creation is replaced with the next one, love will remain,' I said.

'Absolutely, but that's a topic for another time. The point I wish to make is, that Paul's description of love does not emphasise feelings. Whenever he makes feeling statements they are related to what love is not, such as jealousy, being resentful and the like. In his letter to the Colossians he urged the congregation to put on love above all for it binds everything together in perfect harmony.[9] Genuine care, which means to really take the circumstances of another to heart and be tolerant, that kind of attitude will create a harmonious existence in which love will exert its proper influence, according to Paul.'

'So, you suggest that we are all capable of expressing love by doing good. Being aware of that is helpful for it brings a rather different perspective to keeping God's commandments. Everyone is capable of it,' I summed up our conversation. 'But you don't mean to diminish the importance of love as a feeling.'

'Certainly not. That's why I asked you to bring that stuff along.'

I understood that well enough. 'Love as a feeling reveals the nature of God more acutely and personally than anything else,' I said. 'The closer you get to God, the less the act of doing something, like active prayer, really matters. The intuitive and sensory become important. The saints make that clear.'

'That's what I wish to read some examples of,'

Liam responded.

I ignored that for the time being and continued. 'I also believe that the falling in love between people is a dynamic after the very heart of God. Why it happens and how it happens, I don't know. Why to some and not to others; don't ask me. That it can occur is a certainty, as we both know.' I just felt to say that.

We let my comment sink in for a while.

'Yes, I was lucky to fall in love once, though it took a long time in coming,' Liam mused. 'When most intense, love is a very deep desire for someone else and with great mindfulness of the wellbeing of that person. I found out that falling in love is not at all reasonable in that it can be readily explained or controlled. Feelings just take over. You are no longer the person you usually are, definitely not at the start, nor really when things settle down. A big change takes place.' He paused for a moment reflecting on what had happened to him. 'It brings a joy and an ache, which cannot be imagined unless personally felt. Simply, love of this kind is out of this world.'

That was well spoken. It is exactly what had occurred between Liv and me. We were two lucky "bastards" – Australian speak – Liam and I. His observation that the experience of powerful love in a way is out of this world was quite correct. Human love, at a most intense level, allows for a glimpse of what

God's love is like. However, to us people love is an experience, while for God it is a state of being. God *is* love. Our love is always dynamically charged, full of emotional energy. God's love, though the Bible tells us that God has feelings, is always at rest. From God at rest the affections, intentions and intelligence of love emanate. It has a depth and power of unimaginable proportions. I mentioned all this to Liam, who agreed that it had to be so.

'How would Jesus have understood love?' I asked.

'Now that is an interesting question. Let's toss it around a little. As the eternal Son of God in heaven he would have dwelled in love as a state of being.'

'However, once born on earth, love for him became a human experience,' I followed on. 'Still, in human form he would have understood love better than anyone else. Whether as a person he was able to grasp the full reality of love, its divine magnitude in total, we will never know. Though equal with God, he emptied himself and took on the form of a servant, born in the likeness of men.[10] This would have imposed restrictions on his divinity.'

'Yes. Still, his understanding would have been quite extraordinary though,' Liam observed. 'I think that we might get some idea from the information you have in that folder.'

The folder in question held a few versions of mystical encounters that had love as its main experience. In the history of the church it had been recorded many times how a glance at divine love may be obtained by persistence in prayer and reflection. The veil could be slightly lifted. But the initiative for such a revelation rests always with God. A person's own efforts cannot force the issue and is a hindrance to entering into God's presence rather than a help. Instead of a searching engagement, prayer must become a focused non activity, a resting in the presence of the divine. Christians have described this experience in different ways – how an indescribable love overtook their senses. Not Christians exclusively either. All major religions recognise love as the primary force behind existential reality and make mention of divine encounters with love, in their own specific ways.

'So what have you got?'

Liam felt that his research into love needed to include the mystical. He must have been reminded by his own fleeting brush with that kind of experience. Now sought descriptions clearer than he could ever himself have given. I handed him a few pages while keeping a copy for myself.

'Ah, Kabir,' he said.

I was surprised that he knew of him. This mystic and teacher who is revered by Muslims, Hindus and

Sikhs alike. I had included Kabir as an example of insights on love by other religions. The few lines of his poetry are an example in which love unlimited is the ultimate reality. It uses the word truth to signify that reality. Liam read aloud:

> The flute of the infinite is played without ceasing and its sound is love.
> When love renounces all limits it reaches truth.
> How widely the fragrance spreads! It has no end, nothing stands in its way.
> The form of this melody is bright like a million suns: incomparably sounds the vina, the vina of the notes of truth.[11]

'Very nice, Liam said. 'What's the vina?'

'A vina is a stringed instrument of India.'

'Very nice. What else have you got?' When Liam liked a poem he gave the impression that he was drinking it in slowly, like a good red wine. That was the feeling I had that lunchtime at McLaren Vale.

'Richard Rolle and *The Fire of Love*,' Liam mused picking up the next page. I had copied a few lines by this English mystic of the 14th century. What he had heard and perceived during a meditation on the Lord.

An understanding of heavenly spiritual sounds;

> sounds which pertain to the song of eternal
> praise and to the sweetness of unheard
> melody; sounds which cannot be known or
> heard save by him who has received it.[12]

'Rolle called this music the song of love. The
warmth was a quite noticeable heat that he felt during
the meditation. He understood it to have come from the
creator himself. It was as a manifestation of divine love,'
I explained.

Liam just nodded. John Ruusbroec was next. He
lived in Belgium (1293-1381) and was a major systematic
exponent of the contemplative life and mystical path.
He described succinctly the experience of being at one
with God.

> This takes place in the fathomless abyss of his
> love, where we find full satisfaction, for we
> have God within us and are blessed in our very
> being through the interior working of God.
> There we are one with him in love, though not
> in being or nature. Rather, we are blessed –
> and blessedness itself – in God's essential
> being, where he enjoys both himself and all of
> us in his sublime nature. This is the core of
> love, which is hidden from us in darkness and
> in a state of unknowing which has no ground.[13]

God's sublime nature, the core of love, is hidden
from us, Ruusbroec said, and in his writings continued
to explain that the unknowing, that which can never be
known by a person, is an inaccessible light, which is
God's essential being. I told Liam this and suggested
that this core of love would have been accessible to the
man Jesus in times of prayer because of his divinity. The
magnitude of this experience Jesus could not possibly
have maintained in daily life, but its residue would dwell
consciously in his spirit as the noticeable presence of his
Father. Liam and I discussed that briefly.

The next page in the folder quoted my favourite spiritual
lady, Julian of Norwich. She lived in Norwich, England
(1342-c.1423) and her visions have been a blessing to
many. The intimacy of her encounters with Jesus is
worth noting. I had selected two insights which clearly
portray the enormity of divine reality. The first is the
vision of the hazelnut, which like a little ball rested in
Julian's hand.

> I looked at it and thought: What can this be?
> And I was given this general answer: It is
> everything which is made. I was amazed that it
> could last, for I thought that it was so little that
> it could suddenly fall into nothing. And I was
> answered in my understanding: It lasts and

> always will, because God loves it; and thus
> everything has being through the love of
> God.[14]

There is little to add to what Julian's report of the event conveys. The second quote is perhaps even more startling. Jesus explained to her that it is so great a joy to him that his passion brought her salvation, which is his reward and his honour, that the suffering involved is counted as nothing. She then writes an amazing insight that blows my mind.

> I saw truly that if he could die as often as once
> for every person who is to be saved, as he did
> once for all people, love would never let him
> rest till he had done it. And when he had done
> it, he would count it all as nothing for love, for
> everything seems only little to him in
> comparison with his love.[15]

When reading Julian's *Showings*, which is based on visionary encounters and perceptions, it is striking how measured and balanced her writing is. And yet, it includes these quite extraordinary claims. The only conclusion to arrive at is that indeed this is what was revealed to her. This is the nature of love within God.

Liam sat completely absorbed reading the page various times. 'My God,' was all he said. 'I knew nothing about all this, Baz.' It was as if Lady Julian had completely confused him though that couldn't be so. I just left him in another world and stood up to settle the bill for our lunch. It was my turn to pay.

When I returned he told me he had read the last page as well. The one about John of the Cross, who was one of Spain's foremost poets and theologians. John lived from 1524 till 1591. Liam read the first stanza from *The Living Flame of Love* aloud. John used poetry to write down his mystical experiences..

> O living flame of love
> that tenderly wounds my soul
> in its deepest centre! Since
> now you are not oppressive,
> now consummate! if it be your will:
> tear through the veil of this sweet
> encounter![16]

The idea of the flame not now being oppressive refers to the purifying nature of God's love of which John, as author of *The Dark Night of the Soul*, knew first hand. The encounter related in the poem sought to raise John's spirit to its highest point of intimacy with God. His wish was to have the veil that covers the reality of God, one of love as a state of being, torn. Not fully, for that is impossible, but a rent sufficient enough to have a good look. I explained that to Liam. How John describes these encounters was the next quote on the page.

> Such is the activity of the Holy Spirit in the soul transformed in love: the interior acts he produces shoot up flames, for they are acts of inflamed love, in which the will of the soul united with that flame, made one with it, loves most sublimely. Thus these acts of love are most precious; one of them is more meritorious and valuable than all the deeds a person may have performed in the whole of life without this transformation, however great they may have been.[17]

The soul united with the flame of love knows love at its most sublime – speaking in human terms. That is as best as John could describe it to us. Even just one of these fiery impartations outweighs any earthly achievement by a mile. And that is only having a glimpse on what God's love is really like.

Liam rose slowly, as if the MG could wait for a while. On our way home his mind was not on the joy of driving. In fact, he hardly uttered a word. That was fine by me.

'Hey, thanks, Baz. Thanks a mint,' he said when dropping me off at my door. What do you say to that? I thumped his shoulder and bent my knees deeply to get out of this little car so low to the ground. Real friendship is a beautiful form of love.

4

God, the universe and free will; love, sin and God's holiness

WE HAVE MADE A FIRE and are preparing for our next evening meal. I always try to find a spot in the desert that appears little used by other travellers for it means that wood then is easier to find. If we strike lucky and find an oversupply, it is wise to carry that along. The tracks through the vast Simpson Desert can be surprisingly busy particularly during the winter school holidays. I have made sure not to take us on our journey during that time. While prodding the fire a little, I am again reminded of John of the Cross and mention to Jake why the concept of love had been so important to Liam. About his father's mystical experience, that singular brief extraordinary insight he had received.

'So, that's the bridge then,' Jake says after thinking it over.

'What bridge are you talking about?' I wonder.

'We assume that how people experience love is a reflection of what the love of God is like. But why is this idea valid?' Jake answers his own question. 'The validity is found in mysticism. The experience of the beyond, where it aligns with our everyday experiences. They recognised God's presence as love for as human beings they are able to understand the meaning of love.'

He must have been mulling this over previously as a philosophical question. We discuss mysticism a little until our fire has burned through into some very hot coals. I get the shovel out of the car to build a simple bush grill. Make a hole, not too deep, with a sand ridge on both sides. Shovel hot coals into it and spread them out evenly. Next, place an old oven rack with its edge resting on the two ridges of sand. Bingo: the perfect barbecue.

I will grill two thick porterhouse steaks that are kept vacuum packed in the fridge and suggest to Jake that he fries a few eggs in the skillet and heats up a can of beans. With the lid off, the can is placed directly into the hot coals. We shall have a good dinner this evening, as we usually do in fine weather.

After our meal I recommence our discussion.

'Liam's fascination with love was intellectual as well as spiritual,' I begin. 'He perceived that in taking God's love as a starting point, it might be possible to explain the essential nature of our universe and the human condition; theologically and metaphysically that is. He gave it a good shot, I believe. It also helped him appreciate the Gospel better, he said.'

Jake sat back ready to listen to his father's thoughts. I had to be concise and keep focus on the central theme of Liam's ideas.

'Love influences everything. I have mentioned that earlier. That was the underpinning of Liam's approach. To God love is a state of being, Liam concluded and as such God decided to create. Divine love and intelligence were to find creative expression. Why this happened, we don't know. Perhaps love by nature had a need to share beyond the Trinity. Perhaps love at rest in God sought to become love amongst a myriad of beautifully created entities with people being its crowning glory. Anyway, whatever God's reason, the creative act occurred.'

'Eternal love found existential expression,' says Jake the philosopher.

'Yes; the universe came into being. In essence it differs greatly *from* God, but its reality is *of* God. God and the universe are interrelated. The Bible tells us that creation finds its existence by an act of God in the Son. It is in the Son that everything exists and by his command that it remains. Colossians 1:17 and Hebrews 1:3 declare that. The beginning of John's Gospel is very clear on it as well. All things were made through the Son of God and without him was not anything made.'

'So the physical universe is part of God in Christ,' Jake observes. 'The universe is not separate from God.'

'No, and that's a very important point. If not separate from a God, who is love, then we may assume that the love of the Godhead and the love in the universe are actually two manifestations of the same divine love. As I mentioned earlier: eternal love and universal love.'

'But God is holy and perfect and the universe is not.' Jake makes the obvious statement that has confounded many. How can a fallen universe remain to exist in a God who is without blemish?

'Very true. Liam had a response to that, which I will explain soon. First, I would like to make an observation about what is known as the Fall. God allowed universal love to be vulnerable. In the creation story, the primary dynamic whereby to exploit that vulnerability is presented as *choice*. The ability of making choices is central in Liam's understanding of the Gospel and the human condition.'

'Universal love is vulnerable, but eternal love is not. And choice is the culprit.' Again, Jake hit the nail on the head.

'Yes, that is how Genesis presents it.' I slightly modify Jake's observation. 'Eternal love might also have been vulnerable, if Jesus the man, who was the Son of

God, had made the wrong choices regarding Satan and finally the crucifixion. God knows what would have happened then?'

I let that idea sink in for a moment.

'A further point about God and sin,' I proceed. 'Sin is depicted as entering our world through the wrong choice made by moral beings. It infers the idea of liberty, which inescapably is an aspect of what true love is about. Existentially that translates into free will. The liberty to choose, also against love.'

'You mean that if people didn't have a free will, then the nature of God's love would not be expressed as it might,' Jake suggests. 'I must love voluntarily.'

'That's what I learned from Liam.'

'Interesting,' Jake said.

I explain that the moral choice faced in the Garden of Eden foretold the one facing Jesus Christ many years later. The wrong choice brought sin into our world. The right one, by Jesus obeying his Father, delivered creation from sin once and for all. God foreknew that redemption from sin required the Son's sacrifice. This drastic solution did not deter God from the divine act that created all in Christ.

'Nevertheless, for now, we are destined to live under the power of sin,' Jake said 'Orchestrated by a God who supposedly loves us?' He spoke a little sharply. But they were necessary words. It expressed an accusation held by many against God

'I think you summed it up,' I agree. 'That is, when humanly speaking. From an eternal perspective the situation looks more promising. Even though being without fault, God accepts the blame for our situation. It came to a head on the cross. There God, who never did create sin, destroyed its power. That was the plan from the beginning. A quite marvellous New Reality is awaiting us according to Scripture and Christian tradition. Liam insisted that in getting a complete understanding of our existential reality, of the world we live in, the long view must be taken. One that can see beyond our presently dire circumstances.'

Jake finds it difficult to reconcile a God of love with a suffering world. The hurt of senselessly losing his father remains deeply felt. I sense it bubbling up to the surface again.

'Look,' I tell him kindly, 'your dad was a theologian and I am talking theology on his behalf because you wish to know his thinking. Theology is much like philosophy. It concerns ideas, however unacceptable those may be to some. Let's leave value judgments to one side for now.'

'A theory of ideas,' Jake mumbles.

'Yes. All I wish to say about the question of why sin exists is what Jesus told Julian of Norwich, that "Sin is necessary."[18] What gives me personally great comfort is something else that he told her. God will do a great deed. "All will be well, and every kind of thing will be well.""[19]

Jake is noticeably missing his dad right now. He wipes his eyes over with his arm. Talking on will be meaningless right now. I decide to put the kettle into the fire for some coffee, as we often do. The boy's grief hits me and perhaps I should stop our discussion altogether.

'I didn't really know him,' he mumbles. A comment I cannot leave unchallenged.

'Of course you did,' I urge him, making sure to have his proper attention. 'One thing you must understand, Jake. Though Liam was full of ideas and enjoyed the vibrancy of that, what really mattered to him were not ideas at all but people, particularly those close to him and you were the closest. How much can you know at sixteen, when suddenly your dad is gone? Not everything, but still you can know a lot, things much more important than theology or philosophy. You knew what your father was like just fine.'

I leave Jake sitting with his thoughts and get milk out of the fridge. He accepts his cup with a weak smile. 'Shall we stop our conversation,' I suggest.

Jake shakes his head.

'Sorry, Baz,' he offers. 'That's the last thing I would want.'

I tell him there is nothing to be sorry about. After a short time of quietly recollecting my thoughts, in the utterly silent desert night with both of us tentatively sipping at the coffee to avoid burning our lips, I decide to plunge in once again. Not doing so would be the wrong response and unkind to Jake. If I am honest, I would rather have waited. I speak more slowly, with less animation, to tone the conversation down to an easy pace. Jake, I sense, will just be a listener for now, not making comment.

The tragedy of the Fall did not change the dynamic of universal love, I continue. But its influence ever since was to face different circumstances, and very much so. In the creation story, death, decay and evil began a destructive work. Love before the Fall had brought peace to Adam and Eve. But after their choice towards disobedience that changed. Love became noticeably more remote from daily life. Having exploited love's vulnerability Adam and Eve became vulnerable themselves and felt naked. From then on the human experience of love may be described as seeing in a mirror dimly, through a dark haze.[20]

The Fall raises the question of the interrelation between a Holy God, perfect and incapable of sin, and a creation that exists in a sinful state; whether eternal love might have disassociated itself from universal love. Or, has it remained one love with two realities that both exist in God? The fact that after the Fall creation still holds together in the Son, who is divine, must mean creation has not been cut off from the essence of God. Universal love has not been disenfranchised from its eternal source. Love, as it manifests in creation, remains a love that originates with God. This interaction between God and creation is not a one way happening. The experiences of universal love, which include the assaults of sin, are communicated back into the divine realm.

I let Jake sit with that for a while and stop talking. One key observation I must still make. After some minutes I continue.

'The prevailing relatedness of eternal and universal love raises the question of holiness,' I suggest. 'Can God remain holy while being affected by the unholy that occurs in creation? For that to be so, the idea of holiness needs qualification. What exactly does holy mean?'

Liam had his own answer to that question, I tell Jake. The key to it was God's perfection. Holiness means not that God remains untroubled and untouched by the disasters of the world. No, God deals with those situations perfectly in God's love. This perfection, that emanates outwardly, is known as God's holiness.[21] Holiness does not mean remaining unaffected, but being perfect in loving responses. That applied to the man Jesus as well. It must have been his main struggle.

'You know of Aristotle, of course,' I suggest. It is a silly statement as Jake is a student of philosophy. But the question sharpens his attention.

Jake briefly looks at me sideways.

'Aristotle proposed the actual Being of God to be the Unmoved Mover, who dwells beyond the reality of our creation. The very concept gives the impression of disassociation. I make action happen but dwell beyond it. This Greek idea has influenced theology for many centuries and still today. Needless to say, Liam had little time for that. To him there was no need for this kind of abstraction. God is well able to love and be perfect, to be involved and not alienated from creation, in spite of sin. He used to tell a small parable to make this point.'

> God is like an endless eternal ocean charged throughout with love and intelligence. A great calm dictates the crystal clear water but for one murky spot where the water is different. There a powerful disturbance reigns with shapes moving to and fro creating agitation. The calm moves in and restores what was at rest before.

'The disturbance is not separate from the ocean, but contained by it,' Jake observes sensing that I have ended our conversation. He raises his arms, kicks up some sand with his boots while stretching out fully in his chair, and stifles a yawn. It has been quite a day.

5

The validity of faith and theology;
God's suffering love and God's pain

'BAZ, YOU'RE AN ENGINEER, a scientist of sorts, you build big boats: why this interest in God?' Jake asks. Lunchtime had arrived.

His question alludes to the idea generally held that the modern person is self-sufficient. Has little need of religion. It is handy for nice weddings and funerals, and even that idea is diminishing in value these days. Why bother with God? I reflect for a moment on how to answer Jake, for the question is quite central to our conversations. I also sense that he is seeking answers in how to personally deal with the issue.

'You have heard of superstring theory?' I suggest. As a mathematician he would have. The theory consists exclusively of mathematics and explains how our universe might hold together. It is based on pure thought and cannot ever be empirically verified.

'The person considered by many the smartest particle physicist of them all, a man called Ed Witten, thought it the greatest thrill of his vast intellectual life to realise that superstring theory does not simply allow for the possibility of gravity; it demands that gravity exists.[22] This conclusion is like science in reverse. Normally, you would study a phenomenon and then explain the physics. Superstring theory seemingly can arrive at conclusions the other way around.'

I have arrested Jake's attention.

'What I mean is: here is a theory that suggests that because the theory, a purely mental construct, appears to stand up, a phenomenon – in this case gravity – simply will have to exist. That isn't so different from having spiritual perceptions of a reality beyond and concluding that this reality is what brings our world into being. Of course, the scientist mostly works with the language of mathematics, while the religious person uses the language of revelation.'

Jake mulls that over and pinpoints a difference. 'But the scientists have confidence in mathematics related to superstring theory because earlier mathematics had proven its worth in explaining phenomenon that *can* be tested and verified as correct. Finally science then reaches beyond those criteria. Mathematics uses a proven system, while religion uses untested, diverse ideas.'

'Okay. For a moment let's consider the concept of reason,' I respond. 'Take philosophy, which is a discipline that uses reasoning - as mathematics does. Perhaps you consider it a science, perhaps not. Its enormous influence in society cannot be denied. Contemporary philosopher Colin McGinn holds though that philosophical questions like, what is truth and how can we have knowledge of anything, after thousands of years still remain unanswered. The great problems of philosophy are real, he says, but they are beyond human cognitive ability.[23] And yet, philosophy is acceptable to the modern mind even though it seems not to be that effective in what it seeks to achieve. But ideas based on revelation, which likewise involve non-physical reality, are considered suspect.'

'What exactly do you mean by revelation?' Jake queries.

'Revelation is a set of data obtained over many years about what the reality beyond our reality seems to be like. How that reality is relevant to our world. It is historical and has been recorded either in story telling or in writing. Every system of religious belief has written texts these days. The information across the board is vast and quite consistent in its fundamental understanding. We are dealing here with information that has real value and is not simply a figment of imagination. The Christian record is the Old and New

Testament plus data gathered throughout the history of the Church.'

'And you consider that data solid enough to use meaningfully like a scientist would?'

'Yes. I understand that the activity of reason used in mathematics seems very solid because it is basically a coherent system that can be understood. The reasoning of classical philosophy is engaged with far more undetermined ideas. But it's considered worthwhile. In like fashion, it may be said that the deliberations of theology are also worthwhile, second rate to nothing.'

'Philosophy doesn't declare its ideas to be absolutely true though, like religion tends to,' Jake observes.

'Yes, that's a good point. But you must distinguish between religion and the discipline of theology. Christian religion purports to offer truths about God. This 'absolute value' involves a faith component. Theology simply works with these truths, possibly creatively, and need not declare these facts as undeniably true to function properly as theology.'

'Which makes theology like philosophy. It deals with ideas and what it concludes may be correct or not, or perhaps partly.' Again, Jake sums it up precisely. He would have remembered our previous conversation.

'Yes, and there is a quest of course. Science seeks to give The Answer in full to how the universe works though many scientists doubt that will ever be achieved. Liam was fascinated with a similar question: how do things actually work universally and work best in life? He tried to get a handle on it, even if just a very small one, using theology. Suitable findings from other disciplines including science he used as well. His ideas are just an arrangement of possibilities, like philosophy, but that was fine by him. He presented theory.'

'Theology classifies as a science of sorts then, one that uses revelation as its criteria?' Jake suggests.

'Yes, you might say that. Most scientists would hold though that only what concerns itself with physics and testing can be considered science. However, much in theology can be scientific in the general sense in that it deals systematically with language, historical data and human behaviour. It was not the kind of theology that interested Liam. His was mostly philosophical, partially towards an applied theory in human wellbeing. We shall come to that. Plenty of theologians though are simply scientists of sorts. Perhaps they began with a belief in God, but they may have lost it. To them religion is a phenomenon that warrants study. Liam was never like that. It was his belief that made theology a joy to him.'

'Back to belief,' Jake says.

Our discussion seems helps him.

'Yes, and let me ask you a question which you don't have to answer. Why do you find it difficult to believe?

What are the reasons?'

I just let my question sit there for a while and notice a big lizard up a tree branch close by. It is camouflaged very well blending in with the timber. I point it out to Jake, who walks to the car to retrieve his camera. The reptile sits absolutely still basking in the sun. Its profile as ancient as the land we are travelling through.

'That's amazing,' Jake says after taking pictures from all angles. At his last shot the lizard scuttled away. Perhaps a reflection in the camera lens disturbed it.

'The main reason for people being reluctant to believe in God might be a matter of autonomy,' I continue.

'You feel, that you are being told what to do,' Jake suggests.

'Exactly. The information about God is gained from the religious establishment. Soon you find out that you are a sinner, for that is what the rulebook says. Christ can solve that and now you are beholden.'

'Isn't that true then?' The somewhat sceptical tone of my voice surprises Jake.

'Oh yes. But the Gospel doesn't start with the sin bit. It begins with heaps of the love of God towards people. You are being loved! That is the beginning. You are a loved person. The dynamic of sin spoils a lot of things, but you are being loved. So much so that God gave his only Son to deal with the problem of sin. Though we are enslaved to sin and unfit for heaven, God will not blame us for that. The sin bit, the problem that God made sin possible, Jesus has dealt with for us on the cross. We are invited to accept that personally. Indeed, God will hold us accountable for the moral choices we wilfully make between good and evil. That's different. Those choices are our responsibility. And even there Jesus steps in. Liam was quite precise on that. It will be part of a later discussion.'

Jake remains silent, and I continue.

'The religious establishment has a habit of powering it over people. It does this in many guises. You can figure that out for yourself. It tends to hide the reality of God behind cult and tradition. Jesus was very aware of it. His struggle was not with the people predominantly, but with the religious fraternity of the time. I don't think that the situation today is much different.'

'So Jesus isn't pleased with today's church?'

'Often he is and often not, I would say. He barracked for personal freedom and good living - not subservience. Love sets you free! Jesus demands no more than to accept him as Lord to your own benefit and to live a decent life in your own right, in which the power of love, a spiritual power, will help you.'

'So I can be a Christian without the church?'

'In principle that is so. In practice, it is still the church community where the wisdom about God is to be found. There are plenty of good people in the church. Anyway, the final point presently to make is that our discussion is theological. Perhaps it will guide you towards believing, perhaps not. That's up to you. Belief is not essential to understanding the fine thoughts of your father, though it would be a help.'

Jake is driving He had started this morning, and now continues after lunch. He visibly takes pleasure from it. I suspect he has been watching me these last few days – how it is done. One red sand hill after another is left behind us with the next one in sight a mile or more away. I have told him to keep his thumbs not around the steering wheel but against it. That way, if the wheel spins wildly because the tires hit an unexpected obstacle, your hands are not being knocked loose. You keep control of the wheel while it rushes through your fingers. I can see that he is heeding that advice. My mind is mulling over our discussions. Clearly the information is not overloading Jake, who has considerable powers of concentration. Just like Liam had. I have to be selective though in what I share. There are ideas that excited Liam that may be left out for now. Though related to our theme, they are not essential. The main points thus far have been on the nature of love and the notion that all of life issues from love and also the good. That the possibility of choice, wrong choices, brought about the reality of sin with its death dynamic and evil. Good and evil are moral qualities. People must manage those. Love issues from God and in that one love Liam distinguished an eternal and universal quality. Love itself is not a created entity but a divine influence. The effects of love are restricted by sin, but love itself is not marred by it.

There are not two kinds of love in the Son in whom creation finds its being, one created and one divine. But it is one phenomenon in two different realities. Eternal love will never disconnect from universal love even though the latter has become exposed to the assaults of sin. Love divided would be against the very nature of love, which embraces and cares. Love cannot be divided against itself for it will cease to be love. When Liam suggested that to me he was enthused by the idea because it allowed for the next step in his reasoning. Listen carefully, Baz, he said. I remember it well. We were sitting in his study, half neat, half messy, in the easy chairs. Listen, two points. First: If there is no disconnection between eternal and universal love, then it follows that the "experiences" of universal love are transmitted into eternal love. That seemed logical enough. Secondly: When love is exposed to the negative, love is not being tainted by sin, death or evil.

Love remains perfect. Its negative experiences are of pain and grief that someone or something is suffering because of sin, death and evil. This suffering occurs in the reality of universal love and is communicated into eternal love. Did you get that? he asked.

I did and wondered what would be next for he had that smile on his face. The pain and grief of universal love, which can never be separated from eternal love, becomes pain and grief within God, who is eternal love, he explained. Liam's satisfaction was not because the suffering of God is a new idea, but because he had fitted that concept so neatly into his theory of love. He could find real fun in doing theology. Life is a puzzle, he used to say – and so is God.

Many theologians have found making the connection between God and sin such a problem that they kept a separation between the two. Not so Liam. He firmly believed that God's perfection is able to deal with sin perfectly without it affecting God's holiness. Holiness he considered an expression of God's perfection: an action. Apostle Peter encouraged people to be holy in their conduct, as is God who calls them to it.[24] It means to act with the best of intentions. None of us will ever be perfect and we don't have to be, was Liam's conviction. It's our intent that matters.

'If you have a good look at the top of a sand hill you get

an idea what getting over it will be like,' Jake says bringing me out of my reverie. 'If you can see the track made by previous cars clearly it means that the top is fairly firm. When the track sort of disappears the sand is soft. That helps.'

What he means is that it helps you in deciding how fast to approach the summit. With soft sand you need to make extra speed.

'Yes,' I agree. 'Soft sand also slows you down quicker once you are over the top, as you would have noticed. I'll give you a tip for the flat bits between the sand hills. See how you go with that. The track has ruts in it. It varies how many and how deep, but they are always there. The best way to tackle that corrugation is with an even speed. You will have to judge what the right speed might be and then keep at that regardless of what the road looks like. You will find you move over it quite smoothly. Of course, when a deep rut or high ridge appears, you must slow down.'

Jake understands that and has a go. He has a feel for it. The car is a pleasure to drive. Tonight we shall fill up the tank with diesel from the spare jerry cans we carry. Obviously, there are no fuel stations in the desert.

You know that one of my favourite Jewish writers is Rabbi Abraham Joshua Heschel, Liam had said.

I did know. Heschel's little book called *The Sabbath*

makes for exceptional reading. If only we could follow through on what he is suggesting: keeping the Sabbath free for God alone. Heschel writes with a feeling that hints of a divine influence behind the words.

In Heschel's study of the Old Testament Prophets he holds that God stands in a passionate relationship with people and is personally involved in their conduct and fate. This relationship extends to the whole of creation. Heschel called it the pathos of God. It finds its deepest expression in the fact that God can actually suffer with a suffering of deep intensity.[25] I think that is altogether correct, Liam explained. The sufferings of love are love as suffering, I believe.

I asked him for more clarity on that last statement. It seemed rather obtuse. What did love as suffering refer to? Liam continued in saying that the event of suffering to God is always an event of love. Like a mother who suffers over a sick child. Her suffering is a love event. Love is confronted with suffering and love suffers in turn. With God all the suffering in the world becomes divine eternal love that suffers. That is massive, Liam exclaimed, rubbing the back of his neck. Love as suffering is as much love as love as a positive life force is. It is just a different aspect of the same reality.

He had me a bit astounded. I had never thought of it quite like that. What do you reckon, Baz? he asked. Will love ever refuse to suffer? In my language, will eternal love ever tell universal love that it doesn't know of it? Of course not, for in doing so it would surely deny itself. Accordingly, the view that God knows not pain personally cannot be maintained.

I wondered aloud whether that pain changes God, like pain changes people. Suffering does things to you. But how does it affect God? In what manner is pain processed within the Godhead?

He had been thinking about that, Liam said. The question is, can God experience pain and suffering without it changing the essence of God? That has to be so.[26] It is like a cloth soaking up water without it changing the actual cloth itself. Except that with God that water is scalding hot you could say and pain is felt accordingly. Perhaps the cloth is so capable of dealing with pain that the hot water cannot change the nature of that cloth one iota. It has to be something like that. Pain can exist in God without it altering holiness, perfection or any other attribute designated to the divine. Thus God remains the same yesterday, today and forever. It has to be so, Liam concluded.

It seemed fair enough.

The sun is on its downward path and we need to find a campsite for the night. I tell Jake, that he may decide. Soon, we drive a short distance off the track into a beautiful spot.

6

Metaphysics and a relational universe;
Leibniz, Whitehead and Oliver

CITY PEOPLE TRAVEL in the Australian outback for various reasons. Some like to go where they have not been before. Others simply enjoy taking a 4 WD vehicle to remote places for the challenge and the fun of the driving. Most will agree that the open country does something to you. Sitting literally in the middle of nowhere is an experience which you can never get in suburbia. Not everyone finds that attractive. I remember once stopping with Liv on a high lookout in the Flinders Ranges. You could see for miles. It was awe inspiring. A city car drove up fast over the rocky ground. Three young passengers climbed out and quickly looked around. I heard one girl say, let's get out of here, this is boring. Back they jumped in and sped off. Liv and I looked at each other in utter amazement. It was a strange experience for us and an informative one.

Tonight our meal consists of a chopped up onion and green capsicum tossed into the skillet with mincemeat and some oil. Once properly fried I will add a bottle of pasta sauce. Jake is looking after the camp oven, a small cast iron pot, in which he is boiling water to cook the pasta. We will have a simple and nutritious dinner. There is a slight wind that puts a chill into the air. Not fierce enough to blow up sand, fortunately. We are both sitting with our backs into it and have set up the tent likewise. There is no danger of a sand storm today. In the desert the unwary can easily die. It happens every year, usually because people get lost or their car gets stuck. The advice is to carry plenty of water and when in trouble stay with your vehicle. A rescue party will eventually find you. I have hired a satellite phone, which adds to our safety. Every night I inform Liv of our progress. A few times Jake has talked to Sandy.

At dusk we continue our discussion. The light allows for seeing the environment in shades of grey. That will soon finish. The stars are becoming noticeable and will shine brightly within the hour. I tell Jake that if he prefers to give it a miss, then that is fine by me. In turn he asks whether I would like a break. There is no need.

'Metaphysical philosophy,' I ask, 'what do you know about it?'

'That modern philosophers mostly avoid it,' Jake

follows on by giving a good description. 'Central to the discipline of metaphysics is the idea that for a theory to have value it need not be proven, though it must seem plausible.'

'Yes. It's about ideas of an esoteric nature. Those ideas cannot be classified as a proven or testable theory. Metaphysics reasons with non-physical and non-scientific concepts.'

'Like the idea of love,' Jake suggests.

'Yes. The word love is a metaphysical concept when used in a theory of existence, as Liam did. How love might affect every aspect of creation, if one is willing to accept that it does, needs speculation of a non-scientific kind. Such an exercise is by no means mere fantasy and futile. It has value, if made adequately plausible.'

Jake has no problem with that. The world is awash with metaphysical theories.

'Liam understood that the primary forces in our universe, those of love and sin, are relational. Love is easily accepted as the ultimate relational expression, but not so sin. Still, sin is relational; it works on people with destructive consequences.'

'Like abuse?'

'That's but one example, of personal relating. But there is a non-personal meaning to the idea of being in relation also, that of one dynamic influencing something else. Such as sin imposing death on all of creation and love being the source of its life. That is relational as well.

'We live in a relational universe,' Jake again quotes his father.

'Spot on, Jake,' I say. 'The universe finds its origin in God's love. Love is relational. Liam was taken by the idea that the universe functions because of relationality and much to his delight he found some support for it in philosophy. Have you heard of George Leibniz?' (1646-1716)

'Yes, he was a contemporary of Isaac Newton. He maintained that physics and mathematics would come up short in explaining how the universe might function. That is all I know,' Jake admits. 'Something about monads,' he adds.

'Our discussion will be mostly philosophical,' I tell him. 'Quite so.'

Jake just smiles and looks at me. Try me, he seems to say.

'Leibniz was not disenchanted with mathematics and mechanics as science, but in the tradition of metaphysics sought to explain the unified reality from which the universe has issued. He understood that energy, a certain Force, was needed as a fundamental dynamic principle to keep the momentum of the universe alive. This energy, he decided, was to originate from primordial intelligent ideas called "monads."'

Jake nods and is pleased that he remembered about monads. His philosophical training will help in making sense of what I'm about to discuss. Even so, I will try to keep the information as accessible and concise as possible. It should not be a problem.

'These intelligent ideas, these monads, myriads of them, reside in the mind of God, Leibniz decided. They may or may not be actualised in matter. Like thoughts might be translated into something concrete, or might not. However, when a monad is actualised as matter in our universe, when God acts a thought out, that monad will become the energy source of that matter and its determining agent in how it will function.'

'So matter is an actualisation of God's thinking,' Jake says. 'And a monad makes a particular matter function as God means it to.' His ability to be concise in summing up a proposition no longer surprises me.

'Yes,' I agree. 'And our central question, one not to forget, concerns relationality at its most primary level.'

'The relational universe idea' Jake says.

'In Leibniz' system, the monads are interrelated like thoughts are in a mind. Thoughts exist in relation to other thoughts and are not independent of the thought process. Thoughts are relational and thus monads exist in relation to each other accordingly. Matter is the manifestation of monads that exist in relation in that way. There is no direct relation between the different kinds of matter in itself, Leibniz decided, just between their sources of energy – the monads. This point which later philosophers will develop and disagree with.'

'As metaphysical theory,' Jake asks, 'what was its main point?'

'Leibniz' essential contribution to metaphysics is the notion that matter is not lifeless, as Newton suggested, but it is what Leibniz called *ensouled*. Liam's interest was in the relational aspect of this theory.' I threw my empty beer can near the edge of the fire to be picked up tomorrow for our rubbish bag.

'Leibniz, for a long time, was mostly ignored. Only many years later, in the days of Einstein, were his ideas destined to find scientific relevance. Harvard professor Alfred North Whitehead (1861- 1947) used Leibniz for a further exposition of the relational.'

'I know of Whitehead,' Jake responds.

'His ideas have inspired process theology,' I explain. 'That God is affectively related to creation and as a result continually becomes; progressively develops over the time of our history. Liam had no time for the idea of God's becoming. But he liked Whitehead's suggestion that *being* and *relational* are fully integrated. The God who *is*, is fully *related* to what happens on earth.'

Jake has never heard of process theology.

'Whitehead considered the relational nature of

reality to be the cornerstone of metaphysics,' I continue. 'No longer was the relational to be merely an aspect in explaining our universe. Instead, being and relation are integrated.'

'No relationality, no existence,' Jake concludes.

'Yes. But instead of monads, Whitehead suggests "actual entities or occasions of experience," which are transient – very short lasting. The world is made up fundamentally of "drops of experience, complex and interdependent."[27] Key is the word interdependent. It signifies a direct relatedness which is constantly active. This interacting results in events, myriads of them. The material world is the outcome of those events which, being transient, means being in flux. In this way past becomes present becomes future. The universe is always in progress, in the process of becoming. It is not a system of energy that is predetermined.'

'How do you know all this?' Jake asks.

'When Liam mentioned it, I thought it interesting and read up a little,' I explain.

Jake nods his head and continues thinking.

'With Leibniz the monads are internally related and interact in response to the "perceptions" each detects with the other, but matter itself is not. For Whitehead that is insufficient. He suggests that "actual entities or occasions of experience," also called "drops of experience," are both internally *and* externally related.

When these *internally* related "drops of experience" interact, it creates "an event." That event prehends other events, as Whitehead described it. This "prehension" is relationally *external*. "Each individual event prehends all the other events of the world that it knows."[28] And thus, all is relational.'

Hopefully, Jake can follow the scope of this sudden information. I need not worry.

'Leaving technicalities aside,' he responds, 'Leibniz suggested that matter is ensouled but itself not directly inter-relational. In Whitehead's metaphysical theory matter is actually relational in itself – everything is.'

'Yes. But of course my explanation is very brief and basic. To do it justice, you will have to read their work for yourself.'

'I might.'

'So there is a progression from the energy source of matter, the monads, being in relation, as Leibniz posited, to the manifestation of matter in every aspect being in relation, according to Whitehead. There is a further metaphysical step that may be taken, but let's have a breather first,' I suggest.

Jake boils the kettle while I get the tea. Water, beer, tea and coffee are our drinks in the desert and are frequently enjoyed. The stars are bright enough with a low half -moon to make torch light unnecessary. There are wild camels in the desert, plenty of them, originally brought to Australia by Afghans for camel-train transports. They will not come near. Any sign of a car makes them disappear. Even during the day you can hardly sight them. They have learned to stay away from the track to avoid being culled by Park Rangers. We have the place to ourselves, or so it seems. No call of a dingo to be heard, not even from afar. That sense of being altogether alone is just an illusion though. There must be little critters scuttling nearby.

'Just now you said that *everything* is relational,' I continue with a hot cup in my hand. 'That statement has the word thing in it, which means entity. It is where contemporary theologian Harold Oliver comes into the picture. He was not happy that the relational is thought to be between "things." He intended to propose a theory in which the "thing" exists *because of* relationality. The relational is to be the origin of the "thing's" existence. The relational is primary. It is due to relation that monads or drops of experience come about, so to speak.'

'Dad would have been pleased with that,' Jake says. 'God is love. Love is relational. The universe issues from God with relation being the primary reality in which everything finds its being. We live in a universe that issues from relation.'

'You figured that out well,' I commend him.

'I'm beginning to get the gist of Dad's ideas,' Jake says simply. 'Often he told me that the relational was most important in life. Everything else comes second.'

That is true enough. Liam not only talked about that, he lived it. The metaphysical theory of relation assisted him in maintaining an unbroken connection between the relational found in the Trinity and the importance of relationality on earth.

'Oliver is highly interested in science,' I continue after a moment of gathering my thoughts. 'He knows that his metaphysical theory on relation cannot be proven by science, but found support for his ideas from the fact that science these days is talking about relationality. He refers to quantum scientist David Bohm who wrote that "no thing has complete autonomy; every thing has only relational characteristics."[29] For Oliver it is not Leibniz' monads or Whitehead's occasions of experience that are the building blocks of the universe: it is, what he called, *reals* - the actual relational itself. A new paradigm has appeared within the mainstream of physics and metaphysics, Oliver insists. That paradigm is transpolar; that is: relational.[30] For him the relational is not an interaction between two entities, rather it is "relation" in which these two entities find their origin. The two poles between which the relational functions, such as one monad and another, thus disappear and are replaced by *reals*, which are transpolar - beyond polarity. For Oliver the substance *is* the relating.

'So, the question of matter and relationality becomes of secondary importance. The relational itself somehow manifests as matter,' Jake says. 'The relational just is, like God's love just is. It doesn't need another to be itself.'

'You should become a lecturer, Jake,' I suggest. Perhaps that might happen one day. The comment pleases him.

'In this theory, if you replace the word relational with love, and Liam believed those two to be inseparable, what may you conclude about matter?' I ask.

'That love has become matter. That figures,' Jake responds. 'Dad would have liked that.'

I pick up the torch from the ground next to my seat and a small stick. 'Oliver explains his theory that the substance is the relating in a simple symbolism,' I explain. Under the light of the torch to show Jake clearly, I write **aRb** into the sand.

'The **R** is Relation and **a** and **b** are its functional dependencies, they happen because of **R**.[31] In Oliver's scheme the relations do not move, but they are what he calls *pure activity*. Like the concept of being, it just is. But this *pure activity*, when stimulated, can issue *relatio* as a concrete action. That dynamic appears as substance. This action in response to stimulus can be "acting on" and "acted upon", which represent **a** and **b** in **aRb**. But **a** and **b** are inseparable from **R** and are its derivatives always existing simultaneously. It means that **aR** and **Rb** is not a possibility. Ontologically speaking it is the "acting" that is real, the *relatio*, and it results in our reality.[32]

Jake thinks this over. 'You'll have to revisit that one day for me,' he says. But his following comment is spot on. 'So, from a relational universe we now have moved to the notion that relation is a universe.'

'Correct. Whatever exists does so as the expression relation. Thus, Leibniz' and Whitehead's concepts involving internal and external relating become a non-question for the relational is primary to everything.'

'That's interesting,' Jake concludes.

I pause for a moment. The fire is slowing down and Jake asks whether to put more wood into it. I suggest not, for our discussion will soon be finished.

'The theological ideas which Oliver connected with his theory, Liam did not at all agree with,' I continue. 'Oliver sought to build his theory on data gained from "experience," on what potentially can be known. We know about God and that classifies as experience. Beyond it, there is no God for us to know, according to

Oliver. In this way he reduces God solely to the level of human knowing. God belongs to the known and becomes the "Totality of Relations," or rather, we call this totality God. In Oliver's metaphysic the idea of God is a derivative of the "Totality of Relations" and so is the world.[33] Relation is first. As might be expected, Oliver's Christology is questionable as well. Liam had no time for any of this.'

'But he liked the primacy of the relational,' Jake says with a satisfied look on his face.

'He liked it,' I agree. 'He was of the opinion that the relational as a kind of energy is central to everything. The universe exists by it and with regard to human wellbeing love, the most primary and positive relational expression, becomes the key. The connection between love and wellbeing is not a new idea, of course. That he deduced three primary relational principles from the Trinity for people's use in applying love is somewhat special.'

'But that's for later,' Jake assumes, correctly.

7

Jesus the man; reading Scripture with the eyes of love

IT WAS NOT A LARGE CONGREGATION in the
church we visited. The drive up in the MG through the
hills east of Adelaide had been a pleasure. Not often did
Liam preach. I don't actually preach, he was used to
saying. I just talk a little about what I hope is interesting
and may help people somewhat. It was in response to an
invitation by one of his students that he was to address
the Sunday worship service. Liam had suggested that I
come along, to which I readily agreed. He was always
worth listening to. What will your talk be about? I had
asked as we drove through the beautiful hills. About
Jesus, he answered rather vaguely. Liam was not one for
sharing what he was to say before its time. He wore a
pinkish open necked shirt with a faint print on it and
some jeans with a pair of Rossies, quality boots made in
Adelaide. His old well-thumbed Bible lay on the back
seat. His brown hair was a little dishevelled but he had
shaved for the occasion. Liam had what is called a

strong jaw, below a distinguished nose. He didn't like preaching, but he loved talking about Jesus.

When his turn came to address the church he looked at the audience and smiled. I'm here because of Karin, he said, so if you don't like what I will be saying, please blame her. He waved to Karin. Soon you could hear a pin drop. Liam had a knack to make people listen. It wasn't so much what he said, though that was informative enough, but how his easy voice made you feel comfortable, ready for a good ride. Here was a man who had nothing to prove, didn't care much about proving anything even if he could have, and who seemed to be nothing but supportive in assisting you in your Christian walk. Also, he kept his information easily digestible and never alluded to the scholarship that was behind it. But you knew it was there and were happy to take his ideas on board. His theme was that God is love, Jesus came from God to be born a human being, and how Jesus the man might have come to learn about the love of God. Did he just automatically know it, for he was divine as well as human? Liam thought that to be incorrect. As a person things were revealed to Jesus. Jesus learned to walk in the ways of God. But once Jesus understood the magnitude of God's love, how then did he look at the world as he found it? What was he like? Jesus would not have known of his fate as a little boy,

Liam said. You don't burden a child with such matters. Though being in the form of God he emptied himself becoming a human being, Paul writes.[34] I take that to mean, Liam continued, that Jesus, though from a divine and uncreated origin, was firstly a human being to whom his mission and position would be progressively revealed by God. Not much has been recorded about his early childhood and him becoming an adult. We know of his conception and birth plus his presentation in the Temple of Jerusalem, at which Simeon declared in thanks to God that now he had seen the salvation of all people.[35] Again Jesus, according to custom, was at the Temple when twelve years old. He confounded the teachers with his insight and told his parents when they chided him for having stayed behind while they had started travelling home, that it was rather obvious where he would be. It would be in the house of his Father. Still, he followed Joseph and Mary obediently back to Nazareth and over the years increased in wisdom and in stature, and in favour with God and people.[36]

We know that Jesus grew up in Galilee, Liam continued, a pleasant land with open spaces. His would have been a typical Jewish childhood being well cared for and religious. The revelation of his' being a son-ship that found its origin in heaven must have come before the age of twelve, which his answer to his parents about remaining in Jerusalem shows. His engagement with the teachers there displays significant spiritual sensitivity at an early age and good insights into the Jewish religious texts. Only the Gospel of Luke gives this information. The other three Gospels do not find it significant and begin the story of Jesus the man at his baptism. He must have been about 30 years old then. None of the Gospels cover his life between 12 and 30.

Liam sipped some water. It might be considered prudent not to make comment about this period, he said. It is not known when Jesus discovered what about himself, about his Father and his mission. There is no doubt though that over time he gained a complete understanding of what being the Son of God meant, of which the Gospels testify. For how that happened we may refer to Apostle Paul and his explanation that he gained his understanding of the true meaning of Christ through visions and revelations. Paul found himself in a third heaven and in paradise hearing things there that cannot be told.[37] The Revelations of John are another instance of how God communicates spiritual realities, as are the Old Testament prophets. It can be readily assumed that Jesus had similar experiences and those at a spiritual level no other person will ever be allowed to enter. Jesus fully understood the nature of God's love, the abomination of sin and the possibility of a New Creation. That is our Gospel. It became the driving force behind all his actions and teaching.

Jesus insisted on being baptised by John the Baptist. It was not signifying a cleansing of personal sinfulness, which is what baptism meant to ordinary people, but rather entering the journey of a new beginning. His walk as the Son of God was to commence. Jesus would no doubt have been tempted towards wrongdoing during his development into adulthood like anyone else.[38] The preparations of his Father for the task ahead must have been challenging. However, he did not fail. When Jesus rose from the waters of baptism God declared his pleasure with his beloved Son and the Spirit of God descended on the Saviour in the guise of a dove.[39] It appears that the enablement of Jesus was now complete, Liam suggested.

Further temptations, more strenuous than those thus far, awaited Jesus. The test stepped up to the highest level of spiritual obedience. After his baptism the Spirit drove Jesus into the wilderness for forty days and nights after which the tempter arrived. What Jesus experienced during that forty day fast we will not ever know. It fits the Jewish tradition of the great prophets, is reminiscent of Moses and Elijah. Neither of these two men of God faced the Devil though. Only Jesus did, when his fast had been completed. What happened in that encounter you can read in Matthew chapter 4, Liam said. Satan's aim was to make Jesus choose wrongly. The man Jesus, who was God's love personified,[40] was offered all the glory and the kingdoms of this world, if he would decide to bow down and worship Satan. Jesus would have fully understood that this meant avoiding his crucifixion.

Choice is a key aspect in how creation functions, Liam explained. It was because of making wrong choices that creation fell. Once again a person is to choose. But this time the person is as human as Adam and Eve, who is also the Son of God. The encounter between Jesus and Satan was at the highest level of authority. Jesus, the one in whom all has been created in love, against Satan in whose being sin resides in its fullness. Uncreated being in created form, Jesus the Christ, faced the choice that Adam did in Paradise. Not this time in the eating of a forbidden fruit, but the signing away of creation to sin forever. Since Adam's fateful choice people are born and live under the power of sin, are morally deprived. Jesus, though fully human, had not succumbed to this. He knew no sin,[41] and thus the approach by Satan was like the original one to Eve.[42] Once again a choice was to be made, this time as the beginning of the endgame. And Jesus sent the tempter packing. 'You shall worship the Lord your God and him only shall you serve,' he declared, Liam exclaimed with a note of triumph in his voice. Jesus had come to do the will of his Father and none else. It must really have been a tremendous challenge, the scope of which we cannot imagine.

Jesus was God's love personified on earth, Liam continued. The incredible love of God walked amongst us as a man. He was a fine person to be with and a confusing one, as his disciples would testify. He was compassionate and caring, moved by the masses of people who were like sheep without a Shepherd.[43] He had integrity, was never two-faced and took responsibility for the task at hand, a long three years, because of love. His miracles brought the reality of a present God closer to the people, while his teaching astounded them. He had come to herald in a new kingdom, the Kingdom of Heaven and the arrival of the long-awaited Christ. But it was all too much. The world was unable and unwilling to understand this exceptional display of God's presence. It could not handle it. Its mindset and traditions were altogether different. It hit back.

Jesus expected as much. By declaring himself of divine origin and God as his Father, any Jew would have drawn the wrath of the religious establishment. That this was backed up with a display of divine power and the explanation that such was solely in response to the initiatives of the Father, added fuel to the fire.[44] It was infuriating. Never had there walked a man like this.

Jesus understood the true nature of God's love, Liam said. But it was incommunicable. Therefore, he told parables and let his actions speak as best they could. Let's see what that meant.

Firstly, Jesus had no intention to water down, what love might achieve, in order to make it culturally relevant. Such talk would have denied the nature of who he was. Jesus was to be uncompromising regarding the power of love, its potential, and the difficulties involved when aiming for that high standard. He declared all things to be possible to the person who believes in the God of love even though reality will show it might not be that probable.[45] He never backed down in situations where the practice of love was being challenged even though this response meant suffering. Nor did he ever suggest such a retreat for his followers. There would be no compromise. Love was to stand unassailable in the face of the power of sin. The motivations of sin were to be brought to light, particularly so in matters of religious hypocrisy.[46] Nothing angered Jesus more than finding a misrepresentation, a sinful one, of his loving Father. One day, he cleansed the Temple with a whip.[47]

Furthermore, he never shied away from declaring who he was and what he was capable of. Liam gave some examples. Yes, I am the Son of God. I can do miracles and I have power over demonic forces. Yes, I can forgive sins. No, I'm not defiled by mixing with the Samaritans, tax collectors and infidels. I have every right to cleanse the Temple. 'Before Abraham was, I am,'

Jesus declared and thereby made himself equal with God.[48] Jesus had come to establish the Kingdom of God and was an exceptional Prophet. He was courageous and undaunted in the face of fierce religious opposition. He had little time for people who seemed to be too hard of hearing. His main focus though was on giving insight into God's love and advice on how that love should be expressed bringing wellbeing and harmony. In the end they crucified him.

Liam sipped some water once more and seemed to reflect for a moment on which points to make in closing. He said, you don't often hear the full story of Jesus told. We learn about him in bits and pieces from sections in the New Testament broken down in chapter and verse. These verses are then elaborated on, interpretations are given, and theories are built. Of course, the story of Jesus existed well before it was written down. There is so much, it cannot all be recorded Apostle John tells us[49]. When I consider Jesus, as I often do, Liam said, the idea of gaining insights by reflecting on the overall story appeals to me. It seems to make Jesus more real; more complete. It also highlights Jesus the man to me. The question you might ask of yourself is: what idea do I actually have about Jesus? I suspect that quite a few Christians have little idea at all beyond Jesus being the Son of God, being mysteriously somewhere. But what about Jesus the man, who was like us, but more than we are. What about his humanity? May we know him like that? There is a human being sitting on God's throne, someone once said. That's interesting. I become inspired when reflecting on our Lord Jesus. I can recommend it, Liam said.

There are two aspects that seem central to all Jesus was about. Firstly, over time he had come to know God, his Father, exceptionally well. I cannot say completely for possibly his humanity may have restricted a full knowing. Well enough though to intuitively know what his Father would be about. 'When my Father works, I work,' Jesus told his bystanders.[50] That idea challenges me personally to become better at intuitively knowing my Father in Heaven also, Liam admitted.

Secondly, love was the dynamic that motivated all Jesus did. That is no surprise for he belonged to a God who is love. Love cuts to the core of everything. When you ask the question what the world was like from Jesus perspective, you may just as well say, how does it compare with love? It didn't compare very well and still doesn't. So what did Jesus do? He embraced love when it meant suffering and he rejoiced in it when all was well. Throughout his walk he threw a lot of love around. He cared about people and he gave advice. This advice is best understood in finding the motivation behind it, which mostly is love and how it should function. Read up on Jesus in Scripture, what he said and did, and ask yourself: how can I detect the intent of love behind these verses? You should try that one day.

I love this Jesus, Liam proclaimed in closing and added that love is actually a very flexible word – much misunderstood. I have no time today to expand on that flexibility, he said. I will leave a sheet with a few practical notations for you to take home. If you are interested in the three Trinitarian Relational Principles that will help you in knowing what love is about as an attitude and expression, a flyer can be found at the back of the hall promoting a short course I teach at my college. It starts in two weeks' time. For now, thank you for having me and for your kind attention. It has been very pleasant.

I decided to enrol in that course and have never regretted it. We stayed around for a cup of coffee after church and upon our farewell drove the MG further into the hills. Liam knew of a place where we could have a bite to eat. It was an old pub, refurbished mixing old and new, which offered a lunch deal – even on Sundays. The service was good and the food tasty. A light Tasmanian beer washed it down well.

Liam wondered whether I had ever tried to paraphrase or sum up the sayings of Jesus as a statement about love. I admitted that the thought had never crossed my mind. I'll get my Bible out of the car, he said, and I'll show you. He was still animated from his talk, which had been well received. I suspected that the main reason for his animation was his topic: Jesus. Explaining Jesus always lifted his spirits. Soon he sat across from me with his Bible open looking for a certain page. We'll use the Sermon on the Mount, he indicated.[51] At that point our beers arrived, which gave Liam some time to gather his thoughts. He was scanning the verses quickly refreshing his memory. I took a first sip of my drink contently.

The Beatitudes present the potential realities of love in a person's life. Those who know these emotions and practise the actions suggested here by Jesus, are blessed, Liam said. Listen to this. I'll give you the love perspective. Blessed are:

• 'The poor in spirit, for theirs is the kingdom of heaven.' Love is never arrogant or cocksure but careful about my ability to know everything, Liam suggested. It values the sense of being dependent on God for wisdom. That will bring a measure of restfulness into life.

• 'Those who mourn, for they shall be comforted.' Love, seeing the state of the world's affairs clearly, cannot help but grieve. This is a sharing in the sufferings of God, who will comfort the mourner personally.

• 'The meek, for they shall inherit the earth.' Love does not insist on its own way, Apostle Paul writes.[52] It is the humble who truly understand the nature of things and thus qualify to receive creation as their dominion. They know what it means to live truly.

• 'Those who hunger and thirst for righteousness, for they shall be satisfied.' The actions of love are pure and holy and when this is violated it makes one thirsty for justice to triumph. God shall make everything right, absolutely. Just you wait and see.

What do you reckon? Liam asked. I nodded not saying anything quickly. I could see well what he was getting at. Before I could respond he was interpreting a few more of Jesus' sayings.

• 'The merciful, for they shall obtain mercy.' Love seeks to be kind, understanding and forgiving knowing that "here for the grace of God go I." A person with that attitude can count on God's mercy in return.

• 'The pure in heart, for they shall see God.' The love of God is pure and completely void of sin. That is the kind of heart, the inner intention, God appreciates in a person and an intimate knowledge of God will be theirs.

• 'The peacemakers, for they shall be called the sons (or daughters) of God.' Love seeks shalom. Peace for all, wellbeing and happiness. Those who facilitate the reality of that kind of peace qualify as children of God and will be known as such by those people, who are able to discern it.

• 'Those who are persecuted for righteousness' sake, for theirs is the kingdom of heaven.' Righteousness is love uncompromised, a quality the world finds difficult to deal with. Those persecuted because of it may know that their actions are worthy of the kingdom of heaven.

I once did this exercise with all three chapters of the Sermon on the Mount, Liam explained. It wasn't that hard. Here, Matthew chapter 6. I will condense it a little to focus on the main points Jesus is making.

Love is not boastful[53] and prefers not to draw attention. Your Father knows the good you are doing and that should be enough (vv 1-4). Pray with meaning for love is personal and seeks intimacy. It forgives, as you are forgiven (vv 5-14). When you are fasting do not become an exhibitionist, it is not love's way (vv 16-18). Know that the treasures of love are very rich and will draw your heart toward heaven where they reside (vv 19-21). Love offers the light of true understanding that brings wellbeing to your whole person (vv 22-23). But you cannot serve both love and wealth. That kind of double mindedness will not work (v 24). It is better to trust your Father, who loves you. God will supply all your needs (vv 25-34).

Our meal had arrived, two plates with beautiful food. It made me refrain from commenting. Following Liam's example, I dug in. His explanation made enough of an impression for me to attempt this exegesis with a focus on love a few days later at home. If John is called the Apostle of love, then he found a good disciple in this best friend of mine. The seafood pasta was as perfect as that special day together.

8

Satan's foothold in a moral universe;
God's non-arbitrary response and love's victory

DISCUSSION TIME HAS ARRIVED once more. We are camped east of Poeppel Corner for the night. Jake settles into his chair comfortably, happy to listen. I tell him that I will continue in explaining the God narrative in the way I think Liam would have, using his kind of concepts. Jake nods his acceptance.

'Modern science,' I begin, 'makes us believe that one day it will find *The Answer* to the question of life and all will be explained. Many prominent scientists though are far from convinced and consider that simply beyond human capacity. They object to physics and mathematics and studies of the brain as being the only pathway to The Answer. It is seen as it presumptuous. Additional avenues are needed in this quest for truth, they reason; ones that will allow for a more open system of thought. We may not even have discovered those yet. The reality is: the idea of God remains a valid option when probing into the nature of our universe. God is far from dead.'

'You say, the idea of God,' Jake queries.

'Yes. When I say, "God exists," it is a statement of faith. But when you consider God purely metaphysically, leaving the faith dynamic out, it is actually the idea of God you are referring to. God's existence cannot be absolutely proven. From now on though, I will just say God and leave the idea bit out.'

'Excellent.' Somehow that explanation pleases Jake. 'And the source of this information is revelation,' he adds. Jake the philosopher is awaiting my story.

'Yes, it is. Plus ideas from other sources where this is relevant. I'll keep it concise,' I promise. 'If you need clarification, just interrupt. You will do so anyway.'

Jake smiles.

I smile faintly in return. He is good company.

'God is revealed as a threesome, as a Trinity. Its members are Persons with a capital P. They are personal in the sense that people are, but without the estrangement existing between people. The Father, Son and Holy Spirit exist in complete harmony and they are One God. That idea is a stumbling block to many folk. My response is that we are talking about divinity here in which the total unity of three Persons obviously is possible.'

'Dad once said that if you mix the three primary colours of red, yellow and blue together you get brown,' Jake contributes. 'Brown seems one colour, but it's actually three being completely integrated.'

Liam was clever like that.

'We have discussed that the nature of God is love,' I continue. 'And that whatever issues from God will find its origin in that love. Because love is by nature relational, we live in a relational universe.'

'Another point of significance is that the creative act of God occurred in the Son. You may remember: no Son – no creation.'

Jake nods.

'The two realities of love Liam suggested, the eternal and the universal, together remain one love. The divine is eternal love. Creation exists in universal love. There is no disconnect between these two manifestations of love.'

Again Jake nods.

'Alright,' I say. 'Now some new stuff.'

'I need to go for a little walk first,' Jake responds apologetically. He gets up and strides away into the darkness.

Jake is growing a beard and it begins to show. I wonder how long he will persist with it once back in Adelaide. I have known him since he was a baby and watched him grow up together with his sister Rachel, who is two years the elder. He always was a nice boy. An ordinary child with mild manners, who was obviously intelligent. He has the blond colouring of Sandy's Danish forebears, clear blue eyes, and developed Liam's strong jaw. At school Jake was top of the class and very good at sport. His high school examination would have qualified him for any university course of his liking. After some deliberation he chose mathematics and philosophy, which would have pleased his father. Not that long before Jake's exams Liam died. Fortunately, that did not affect his results. Now years later, I have the fortune of us being fellow travellers in remote Australia.

I reflect how at lunchtime we had reached Poeppel Corner. An iconic spot on the track we are following. It is where the boundaries of three States in Australia converge. The South Australian northern border running east/west meets the Northern Territory and Queensland ones. At Poeppel the border between those two States commences northwards. A short walk led to a lookout and the current border post which is situated at the eastern edge of Lake Poeppel. The lake is usually dry and only fills up when it rains heavily up north. Originally, in 1830, the post was placed in the middle of the lake until modern survey methods determined it was 1000 feet too far west due to the survey chain having lengthened because of use. A new post, the one we visited, was put in place in the correct spot. At the beginning of a short walk to reach that post, a ledger is placed in which to write your name in as proof of your visitation. The ledger is full, with names scribbled all over.

We had Poeppel to ourselves and decided to stretch our legs this lunchtime taking a few camera shots instead of discussing Liam's ideas. An abandoned spare wheel with a brand new tire lay deserted against a rock. It must have fallen off a car. It is wise to carry two spares in the desert with the second one often roped down onto a roof rack. Ours is in the tray. The wheel is the wrong size. I would not have had space for it anyway.

Leaving the Corner we had driven down the bank onto Lake Poeppel's dry surface and followed the edge facing north just inside the Northern Territory border. A little later we climbed back up the bank turning east into Queensland, direction Big Red. It is the largest sand dune we will encounter and a famous one.

During that drive, I reflected on what we were discussing right now. About how to explain the Gospel as metaphysical philosophy, which is what much of theology really is. The aspect of faith will be left out. Faith is essential, Liam would say, but often we focus on the faith component without ever getting to the beauty of the full divine plan. For Liam, that beauty consisted in the Good News as a coherent story, a love story in fact, with a beautiful ending. I know mine is just a theory, he often said, but to me it is a meaningful one. Obviously, I cannot solve the mysteries of life, he would admit. Still, having a crack at it is nice. It makes you see new perspectives.

That was Liam to a tee: always reflecting on new ways in understanding God.

Jake has settled back into his chair.

'About the functioning of our universe,' I continue, 'Liam wondered how to classify love as being primary to everything. Would it be a force, a power, an influence or a dynamic? None of these describe metaphysically what love really is in his scheme. These terms all are a derivative of love. In the end he decided on the term by which he had called the idea all the time: universal love.

'So, universal love is what *reals* are in Oliver's design,' Jake observes.

'Yes. But the relational in Liam's metaphysic is an outflow of that love.'

Jake nodded that he got the point.

'We shall now look at aspects of God's creation. At its most significant, it features life. There is angelic life and the pinnacle of life on earth is the human being. Both are the result of universal love. The crown of the creative effort is beings with attributes similar to God's own such as emotion, intelligence and free will. The will is free because that is the nature of love: it seeks to be creative and will not enslave. This resulted in the ability to choose, an ability that was to create havoc in the heavenly realm, as well as on earth.'

'Like Star Wars,' Jake suggests with a grin.

'Something similar.' I appreciate that light note in our conversation and will keep it as uncomplicated as possible.

'We have discussed sin,' I say. 'Liam considered it secondary to universal love. Sin is a force that is able to assault universal love and its derivatives such as the good, the force of life - the whole of creation in fact.'

'It can destroy, but cannot issue life,' Jake suggests. 'Consequently, it's secondary.'

'Excellent.' I take a look at him. My face must show pleasure at his contribution.

'I have thought about our discussions,' he simply explains. 'It's interesting.'

'Keep it up,' I suggest, which undoubtedly he will.

'Liam considered the effects of making wrong choices. In the heavenly realm those effects are different from those in the universe. Satan and every angel following him were changed in their very being into evil by their disobedience, but the heavenly realm itself appears not to have fallen like our one did. We don't know much about the heavens which, by the way, are created and also exist in the Son of God. Liam kept his focus on the existential reality that is ours. He asked the question: Following the Genesis story, why here on earth did the Fall reach beyond Adam and Eve with sin infiltrating everything?

'Let me think,' Jake interrupts. For a short while he sits motionless in deep concentration. Jake likes puzzles of a conceptual kind. 'Don't know,' he admits after a few minutes. 'What did dad come up with?'

'Liam found the answer in the word "good." Upon completion God declared our creation to be very good. It was a manifestation of goodness through and through.'

' And good is a derivative of love,' Jake says.

'Yes. Existentially so. Good is a primary derivative of universal love. The relational, the good and the force of life, these are primary in Liam's theory.'

I pause for a moment and continue.

'Liam reasoned that the good was violated by Adam and Eve and that this reached right back into the fabric of the whole of creation for the good is at the heart of it. This violation changed everything. It allowed sin an entry into every aspect of creation. The wrong choice made by Adam and Eve was a moral one. Morality from now on would have to wrestle with sin, rather than solely being faced with the simple question of shall I obey God or not. Morality is relational by nature. You may thus conclude that the relational was violated by sin. The bad choice made by Adam and Eve allowed for sin to infiltrate as a determining power in what our relational universe, that exists in love, would be like.'

'So universal love got a monkey on its back, so to speak,' Jake suggests.

'Very much so. Liam was faced with the question of whether to consider sin a derivative of universal love. He could not accept such a derivative. Love cannot be the origin of sin. But it's a vicious parasite, he often said. Somehow sin got a legitimate foothold in our creation and can suck the life out of it.'

Jake gives that some thought. 'So now we have love, life and good - plus sin, death and evil - opposing each other in every aspect of creation. Life is experienced like that,' he concludes. 'And dad put that into a metaphysical theory.' Jake seems quietly proud of his father and I give that some time. We sit together in silence for a while.

'Shall I boil some water for coffee?' he asks. Apart from talking it is our only real activity every evening.

'Sure,' I reply. Coffee is a good idea.

The night, once more, is a quiet one. I spoon coffee into our jugs under the light of a torch and take milk out of the fridge. A wave of tiredness washes over me, which I ignore. Travel and weariness go hand in hand when on a demanding trip. In a way it is good to be tired – the reason for it. A welcome change from the stress my job tends to bring. I love the desert, the open spaces with a harsh but distinct beauty. There is nothing quite like it. After a few years of good rains the bush looks healthy with new green on its vegetation. That is not always so. We take an easy time with our drinks.

'How will universal love get the monkey of its back, as you have called it?' I continue.

Jake sits staring into the darkness, but is listening.

'The Gospel explains just that. The vulnerability of love, which is choice, had been exploited by heavenly and earthly beings. The heavenly beings went wrong with their eyes wide open. As a result Satan and his demons became sin personified. The earthlings though had been deceived into their disobedience. They were told that in knowing good and evil they would be like God, while having no idea about evil; that it was completely alien to God.[54] That is a lesser crime and perhaps the reason why they, and our creation, remain connected to the power of love after the Fall. As predicted, their choice introduced Adam and Eve to the state of knowing good and evil.

According to Scripture people will be given a second chance to exist in love exclusively. But for that to become possible the power of sin somehow had to be destroyed once and forever.'

I gather my thoughts.

'The solution could not be arbitrarily dictated from heaven – God solving it with a word of authority. The legitimacy of sin needed undoing by love being more powerful in the realm of sin, which is the created realm. Universal love had to assert its superiority over sin by its own power, without the arbitrary involvement of eternal love.

'In the Genesis story, it was the wrong choice that led to devastation. It signified that through a right choice creation could be redeemed from sin in future. In Paradise two blameless people failed and became burdened. A blameless person was needed once again. This time to face a choice that could unburden creation. The way sin entered, it will exit – by human choice. But where to find a blameless person?'

'Then Jesus arrived.' Jake is listening intently. This is not how he has heard the Gospel told before.

'Yes. The One in whom all has been created and holds together, is born a baby.'

'How can you explain that in metaphysical theory,' Jake asks, 'taking love as primary?'

'Liam asked the same question. He decided that the divine aspect of the Son of God being born a child was a mystery beyond human comprehension. However, using the idea of eternal and universal love being *one* love, he decided that those two loves being present *together* in a person should be possible. In fact, they are so within the Son of God for universal love exists in him as does eternal love. That the Son's Personhood would change from divine to human need not severe the connection between these two realities of love, Liam thought. Thus Jesus could be both divine and human. In becoming one of us he had to empty himself of his divine *stature*, as Apostle Paul explains.[55] But in doing so he kept his divine *nature* and there would be no reason why creation could not continue existing in him.'

'Okay,' Jake comments. 'I can see the value of that, though it remains a mystery.'

'Yes. And Liam's ideas are theory, as he was used to pointing out. It brings an interesting perspective though to many questions the Gospel raises.'

'Like, Jesus and sin,' Jake suggests.

'That's the key one. Jesus was subject to the physical power of sin, such as death, hurt and pain. However, he remained blameless with regard to the moral power of sin, which presents in the negative things we do. At its most severe we call that evil. Jesus was as tempted as we are, actually more so, but he never succumbed.[56] Again, we arrive at the matter of choice. A bad choice brought the Fall, continually good choices by Jesus right through into the crucifixion secured the overpowering of sin.'

Jake knows enough about the Gospel story to make sense of that.

'Paul explains that Jesus who knew no sin was made sin so that now we could be made right with God.[57] That cannot mean that Jesus in essence entered the state of sin for then he would have lost his divinity. The nature of God and the nature of sin do not mix. So what was it in Christ that was made sin? Not his divine nature so then perhaps his existential nature? However, that leads to a major problem. Was Jesus on the cross to become a kind of Satan, sin humanly personified in creation? But he was the exact opposite, being the blameless person who would overcome Satan. Liam concluded that the answer was to be found in the idea of a scapegoat. The burden of sin of the whole universe would enter Christ's being like an unimaginable sickness, a power of death which he needed to overcome. And he did. For finally he died not from that sickness, but by committing his spirit to his Father once the job was done. Jesus, the human being, had conquered.'

'Who was also God,' Jake observes.

'He was, but on the cross his divine authority was to no avail. Possibly, that is revealed by him crying out at his crucifixion as to why his Father had forsaken him, feeling alienated and alone. All his divinity achieved was an ability to suffer more deeply as a person than anyone else could have.[58] It was the power of his humanity, of moral responsibility, that counted. Human choice had brought on the Fall, human choice would need to rectify that. Jesus and Satan met on a level playing field. They faced off in the created realm; Satan being fully evil and Jesus as a member of the human race. People, as perhaps you may remember, are the only beings in all of creation in whom good and evil coexist. They have the ability to wilfully choose towards either. How did Jesus win? In the deepest of agonies he kept his choices towards what love stands for. Liam believed, that whatever Satan threw at Jesus, and it was beyond imagination, love embraced and gobbled up painfully without retaliation and without Jesus for a moment disowning his Father, who had presented him to become crucified. The authority of sin became absorbed completely into love and was rendered totally powerless against Jesus the Christ, the perfect human being. Love achieved by suffering, what it would not arbitrarily dictate.'

That will suffice for today. The sky has become slightly overcast, which might mean rain for tomorrow. None is forecast, fortunately. Off-roading in mud is not a pleasant experience. Not only does it spoil camping, but wet dirt from the desert sticks like glue to the undercarriage of a car. It throws up a blanket onto the rear end as well, where driving draws a vacuum. Everything gets filthy. You slip and slide on the track, which may seem fun initially, but the joy soon wears off. Some off-road enthusiasts revel in the mud. I prefer the weather like it has been thus far. There is a second part to the gospel story. It will have to wait till tomorrow, at Big Red.

9

Love's New Reality; Two sides to Paul's Gospel
and the personification of grace

BIG RED IS THE SAND HILL PLAYGROUND of off-road enthusiasts. Every bucket list features it as a to-do experience. Its location is about 20 miles west of Birdsville. It is the last serious sand hill on our trip and the most intimidating. With the western climb, which we are facing, being more difficult than the eastern.

Earlier we had crossed Eyre Creek easily. It can flow deeply and then is difficult to traverse, if at all. The creek is lined by large gum trees, the first large trees we have seen for days. We walked a fair way up the dry bed over rocky ground avoiding sizeable branches thrown about when the creek had been heavily in flood. The sound of birds, which you will not hear in the desert proper, was refreshing. Life was taking a more conventional turn again, at Eyre Creek.

Jake has been enjoying the bush. He has a feel for it and that gives me pleasure. The strain of city life well and truly left him some days past. He has taken to our style of camping, likes the outdoors and adapts easily. Sleeping in a tent or swag in the outback brings you close to nature, more so than anything else.

The distance between the sand hills has increased lately and on the horizon we can now see the last one: Big Red. It stretches for miles north and south showing a sparse vegetation of grasses with a wide section of red sand marking where we will try to get over the top. From afar it may not seem enormous, but once up close that idea soon changes. I can feel Jake's excitement rising. He likes off-road driving and bemoans the fact that he cannot afford such a car. I have asked him about tackling the hill after me, whether he was interested, and got an eager acceptance. Big Red is impressive.

Most drivers eventually get over it, though there is a detour available some miles south. Much depends on your car and technique. The trick is to build up enough speed before reaching the very loose sand near the top. There are three tracks by which to climb Big Red. The extra difficult one I don't think has ever been conquered. There is a middle track and the easiest climb is to the right of that. That still requires a mighty effort, straight up and over. We will take the middle approach, which is longer and veers slightly to the left and then near the summit to the right. Hold on, I tell Jake. Get a feel for how it's done.

I have stopped on the flat near the bottom of the hill. Our car has not been designed to steadily climb up and keep momentum all the way, like some. It has no modifications and is just overall capable. I must make sufficient speed as quickly as possible. That becomes quite difficult once we hit the ruts made by others making the attempt. Ruts have been a problem with many of the previous hills also and are no surprise. We skittle and bounce and jump about while I keep a firm grip keeping the car straight. Our speed is increasing, but will it be enough? Near the top, in really soft sand, momentum drops away. I sense, we might get stuck. The diesel engine grinds on, is threatening to stall, but never does and pulls us through. Throughout our trip the gearbox has been in low range and now it shows how suitable that is. Jake's eyes glitter and he punches the air with enjoyment. I am having great fun myself. We step out to take a breather. What a day!

Reaching the top of Big Red offers a surprise. On the other side is a narrow lake that runs along the bottom of the hill for a long stretch. There are water birds and it is a beautiful sight. We will camp near that lake tonight. But first Jake will tackle Big Red. On our way down the dune I tell him that the key to success is how he manages the ruts in the track. Go too fast and the wheels will bounce and spin uselessly. Slow down too much and you will lack speed near the top. It is not the first ruts Jake will face. He would have noticed that they are a problem as you are descending a sand hill as well. They can shake a car incredibly. The way down Big Red is quickly covered, but confirms how long this climb actually is.

Jake turns around on the flats and sits for a moment facing his challenge. The adrenalin is pumping. If we fail, it will be a matter of reversing. Made difficult because the canopy over the back of the car blocks the rear view mirror. It leaves the side mirrors only. I need not have worried. Jake is successful, but only just; same as I. We decide to have a beer right there, on top of Big Red, celebrating our triumph and enjoying the fabulous view.

Down again, but on the eastern side this time. In places the car slides on in the sand till the track bottoms out near the lake. We select a spot for camping not far from the edge. Close to where the track to Birdsville enters the area. I ask Jake to set up the tent while I take the air compressor out of its bag. Throughout the desert the tires have been on 15 psi. Reduced pressure spreads the tread longwise allowing for more surface contact.

Someone once told me that a lady was found perished in the remote outback because her wheels got stuck in sand. The rescue people needed to do no more than let enough air out of the tires and drive that car out of the ditch. With firmer ground ahead tomorrow I increase each tire till about 30 psi, not soft but flexible enough to absorb the heavy vibrations from dirt roads. Having finished our chores we climb back up Big Red again, by foot this time, and spend a fair while on its sandy ridge. To the north from where we made the crossing is the high point with a fine vista either side of the hill. The lake continues out of view. The sun is dropping in the west, which changes the colours of the desert progressively. The red centre of Australia is quite a place to behold. An engine sound in the distance alerts us to visitors. The noise increases once their car begins to climb. Some folk have driven up from Birdsville to have a look at the sunset. By the time we have cooked our evening meal, they have long departed.

The evening is beautiful and without the breeze that has kept us company the last few nights. Some cows graze on the other side of the lake. There is a cattle station nearby. The water birds have settled in for the night well away from the shore. Trees are a black silhouette against the water that begins to reflect the evening sky with stars yet undefined. Stillness and calm descends all round.

This is the bush at its best: majestic, sparse and undisturbed. I will forever find that awe inspiring. God had made things very good, is the thought that crosses my mind. Things are destined to be even better still, one day.

Jake is never boisterous, but right now he seems especially restful and content. Neither of us feels much like talking. And yet, our environment is ideal for what I have to explain, the second part of the Jesus story. Shalom, Jesus had said, when he appeared for the first time to his astonished disciples after his death: be at peace.

Jake must have read my thoughts. 'Just talk, Baz,' he says. 'And I will listen, gratefully.'

'Liam was of the view that the church reaches beyond Easter insufficiently. It tends to get stuck at sin and the resurrection, he used to tell me. Certainly, the crucifixion event is pivotal in the history of creation. Without it, Christianity would be in vain, Apostle Paul declared.[59] Let's have a look at Easter in its *full* potential.'

Jake settles in.

'The event is mysterious to say the least. Incredibly, Jesus after his horrible death rises as a new person of a different reality from our own. He is the first being of that particular kind. His followers were astounded, naturally. Liam wondered whether to continue applying his ideas to this new and surreal development and saw no reason not to. After all, he decided, it remains the story of love; the love he has been describing.'

'The new Jesus wasn't some kind of angel?' Jake queries.

'No. Not at all like an angel. It is a New Reality that presented itself, which is difficult for us to imagine. Jesus appeared amongst his disciples obviously a person. Someone who could be touched. But he arrived suddenly inside a locked room.[60] He joined them at other times, but they didn't recognise him.[61] Eventually, they came to understand that they were invited into that New Reality themselves. Potentially any person is. Jesus had predicted that during his walk before the crucifixion, but nobody could understand the implications.'

'You must be born again.'[62] Sunday school has left memories with Jake.

'Yes. To be born again means that you enter the New Reality. You become a new creation, though the old one still persists.'

'You have a double identity,' Jake suggests.

'More exact; you become two identities integrated into one and indivisible,' I explain.

'The one is physical, the other spiritual?'

'Not quite. Every person is physical and spiritual.

The transformation into the New Reality means that a new dimension has been be added to the spiritual side of personhood.'

I pause for a moment to give Jake time in absorbing this information.

'How did dad deal with this?'

'Weighing up the information given in Scripture, he decided that the victory of Jesus meant that universal love was no longer beholden to sin. The monkey, as you called it, had lost its grip. With sin fully defeated, God creates in Christ once more. Again in universal love – a similar but different creation to our own. Similar in that it contains people and reflects the world we know. Different in that the substance of the new creation is altogether unlike ours. Both creations exist in universal love, Liam concluded. The new creation is a different manifestation of it. Universal love now presents as two realities, or even three. If you include the spiritual world of angels and demons. All of these are created entities that exist in universal love, the source of creation. Consequently, they are interrelated.'

'Like multiple universes,' Jake suggests.

'Yes. Modern physics considers multiple universes plausible. Quantum theory points that way. Scientist have their doubts about it. Liam did not see that as relevant to his theology though.'

'I can see dad's reasoning. But how do you fit the

process of being born again into it? It's otherworldly and yet it seems to be existential?' Jake the philosopher is attending to our discussion.

'Born again, a metaphysical idea, must be personally embraced. Not merely intellectually but from the heart. As Scripture tells us. Liam found this possible through the human ability to have faith. Interestingly, faith is a choice, a decision you make, based on intuition. Once again, the word choice presents in crucial moments of self-determination.'

'Choice changes your life,' Jake observes.

'Yes, in the form of faith, choice even allows you to enter the born again experience. Faith is a response that involves trust. You believe in information presented that is beyond your faculties of immediate perception. That a faith response towards God can introduce an essential change into your life because of an action of God, Liam had no trouble with. The idea is fundamental to Christian theology. Metaphysically, the possibility of being born once more simply needs to be accepted as a revealed fact, he reasoned.'

'So, existential reality can change because of faith,' Jake offers.

'Yes. You step out in faith towards God, who will respond within your person. How much that step really matters to you is shown by your corresponding actions, your continual choices. You can fake having faith, or it never really takes root and thus becomes questionable. You could become a hypocrite.[63] Faith is very personal and the quality of it is for Jesus to appraise. It is easy for people to be fooled by those of dubious faith.

I pause for a while. Jake is smart enough to figure the choice facing him personally. How to deal with faith in his life.

The lake has darkened into a shimmer of night light.

'What about the church not getting past Easter?' Jake kicks our conversation along.

'It concerns the potential of the New Reality, which Liam considered insufficiently explained to believers. What do we know about this new creation of God? It exists in the Son of God as our present one does. God has reversed the creative process and begins rather than ends with a person this time: the resurrected Jesus. Eventually, the whole of creation will be renewed.[64] Right now we are at the point where two creations are interwoven, one fully developed and in sin, the other taking shape and untouchable by sin. The first will end one day, the latter lasts forever.'

'What exactly do you mean by being interwoven?'

'Consider being born again, not physically as a baby, but of the spirit this time. The event is real in us, but we cannot see it. Two types of creation become interwoven, the old and the new: a life in sin and life without that. Because both types of life originate from universal love, there is no reason why the old and the new shouldn't exist together within one person, Liam reasoned, and do so in a fully integrated manner. With the new having its effect on the old.'

'But we don't hear enough about the potential of that, dad thought.'

'No, we don't.'

I could do with a drink and ask Jake to check how many beers are left in the fridge. None apparently, so the choice is tea or coffee. No fire tonight, as wood is scarce around Big Red. This camping ground is used often, with everyone scavenging for loose timber. Amazingly, we are the sole occupiers at present. The mild evening makes the lack of a fire more bearable. I have pulled out our gas bottle earlier on. Jake indicates that he will do the honours. A green tea suits me nicely.

'Liam recognised two parts to the Gospel of Paul. First Paul's legal/prophetic presentation of God's salvation plan. The second one concerns its new creation aspect.[65] The first is presented best in chapters 1-7 of Romans. Paul's legal gospel explains why we all come short of the glory of God because of sin. The way out is to believe in Jesus and be declared righteous; forgiven and in right standing with God. Sin remains a problem though in life and we will keep struggling with it. Fortunately, we can count on the help of Jesus.[66] Sin will not have the final say over us, as we are living under grace.

'The words grace and mercy are central to Paul's explanation. Mercy is the bestowal of undeserved merit, of being considered worthy regardless. In salvation this gift of love comes from the Father. Grace is that merit. It transforms into a practical influence, which has two sides. There is a state of grace, which means being forgiven. I live under grace rather than law.[67] The word justification is used for this. Then, there is grace as an influence, an enablement by God to meet life's challenges.'

I take a look at Jake. He is staring at the ground just ahead of his feet and seems completely relaxed.

'The church has a lot to say about the sinner and our struggle against sin, plus the way out. That way out firstly is by Jesus Christ and then what the church has on offer, it tells us. There is no problem with that, but it's not the full story. To many believers Jesus is mostly the one to believe in for securing a heavenly destiny. He is some sort of helper in the sky.'

'But he is more than that.' Jake wonders.

'Yes. Many Christians prefer Jesus to be someone close enough to rely on, but not so near that he interferes overly much in everyday life. It denies the true Gospel.'

'So, that is a choice they make,' Jake suggests.

'Not necessarily. They may not know any better and are unaware of the full potential of their salvation.'

'Which Paul explains in the other part of his gospel?'

'Yes. It concerns the personification of grace.'

'Grace becomes personal?'

'Yes. And personal means relational of a particular kind. Not merely a state of being in relation to God, but an active relational divine force in our lives. Liam felt very strongly about that.'

I remember him grumbling about the overly sin focused message of the church. He was rather animated. Sure, sin and its solution are important, very much so. But why get stuck there. Jesus has dealt with it on the cross. We are forgiven. We can rejoice. None of us are perfect, but so what when you are doing your best. God seeks to uplift us, not to keep us burdened us with guilt. I don't know who came up with branding the Christian as a sinner saved by grace, Liam regularly lamented. That is true enough. Paul says so. But it's no longer true as a state of life for me. I am divine grace personified and no longer enslaved to sin. That's who I am. That is how I want to feel; and God help me, that's exactly how I feel. He grumbled on for a while repeating the point in various ways. This was classical Liam. Digesting an issue and chewing it over well. I sat there quietly with a smile on my face. It was a wonderful experience.

'Liam was pleased to think that his theory of love would have predicted the personification of grace. Of course, his ideas were developed while that was already a known fact.'

Jake likes that and asks whether he can have a go figuring it out. That is fine by me. I recommence looking over the lake detecting some black swans, motionless in the water. They are difficult to spot in the dark. It reminds me of Karl Popper and falsifiability. The idea in science that for a theory to become acceptable it must be include a consideration of what could make it not so.

'I think, I've got it,' Jake announces. 'God is love and love is relational. God is also personal, always will be. So, wherever love is expressed without the restriction of sin God is relationally involved in Person.' He looks at me with raised eyebrows awaiting my response. I give him thumbs up and a big smile.

'In Paradise God walked with Adam and Eve. But after their disobedience that changed because love no longer reigned exclusively. In the new creation, that is presently unfolding, love rules without restriction. In the first part of Romans, Paul introduces grace as the power that will reign against sin in support of a holy life.[68]In chapter 8 though, in which Paul begins to introduce

God as the believer's Father indicating familiarity, they being sons and daughters of God, the power of grace becomes personalised. Grace is now described as life in the Spirit, in the Holy Spirit.[69] The Holy Spirit dwells in the believer and it cannot be more divinely relational than that, Liam would say.'

'And you would expect that to make a real difference to a person,' Jake suggests. 'That new power in your life is what dad was referring to.'

'Yes, the power of grace, or life in the Spirit, is an enablement. It can make a big difference, if you learn to tap into it. Paul mentions grace in all his benedictions.'

'How do you tap into it?' Jake wonders.

'It has a lot to do with your communications with God and the choices you make. I cannot go into that now.'

'Dad's theology seems a pretty coherent system,' Jake concludes pensively.

A measure of sadness comes over him and it stirs in me a mix of emotions. The dark outline of Big Red is a timeless presence, somehow rather comforting, rising up impressively behind our tent. Jake takes an early night and finds his sleeping bag. I remain seated in my chair looking out into the quiet darkness over the shimmering lake bathed in moonlight and reflect on what I will tell him at Birdsville. About his father's Trinitarian Relational Model. We are running out of time to discuss that in detail. I will give Jake an outline tomorrow and send him Liam's notes with some comments once back home. I remember those two evening lectures well

10

Postmodern relationality; Imago dei;
A relational Trinity and the creation story

LATE BECAUSE OF ENGINEERING DUTIES, I parked my car behind the college and walked to the lecture room. I did not usually come here as Liam and I kept friendship and work well apart. In all the years of my acquaintance with ship building, including destroyers and sub marines, he never once requested a visit to the yard. One day, when Sandy and Liam had taken a lunch tour by boat on the Port River in Adelaide, they motored past our large complex that builds and assembles ships. They noticed a sub moored for repairs. The facilities are capable enough for the USA to show interest in having its non- nuclear Asian military fleet maintained in our docks. Liam concluded that my workplace was more impressive than he had first imagined, but made no further comment. That was fine by me. Now I entered the back of the room where he was well into a lecture. I was familiar with the gist of what he would explain: that the relational is the essence of being and that good relating fosters wellbeing. But what are the primary principles of that relating? How do we know we are doing okay? I was looking forward to his explanation.

The lecture had progressed past its introduction and was addressing the level of interest in relationality in general. Liam was telling a group of about 20 people about the Relationships Foundation in the UK, with an associated organisation here in Australia. It seeks to inform about the importance of the relational in society. A once prominent Australian cabinet minister wrote in a book of his that, "The depth and quality of our relationships determines the strength of our society and the quality of our lives."[70] It places the relational at the forefront of social cohesion, Liam said. It is now believed that our personal identity also is significantly determined by relationality. Postmodern identity is predominantly social, in which the self finds meaning in the interaction with others. Liam quoted Stanley Grenz, that this kind of self "is highly decentred and fluid, as a person can have as many selves as social groups in which he or she participates." It results in an unstable impermanent self.[71] The modern person, Liam continued, derives a sense of meaning primarily from relational interaction, from being concerned about others and the environment. While authenticity involves doing so adequately and seeing that effort reciprocated. The feeling of how one is perceived by others rates significantly. The Western world has become consciously relational much more than it ever used to be. You may have noticed that yourself with the internet, he suggested.

The word *relate* in its present connotation began with the expression of *having a relationship* in reference to *an affair of a romantic or sexual nature*, and was used for the first time in 1944. That is very recent. The idea of *I can relate to that*, in the sense of feeling *connected or sympathetic to*, was used first in psychological jargon in 1950. Being in relationship due to kinship dates from 1744, while in the mid fifteen hundreds to relate meant to *tell or to recount*.[72] Today's use of relate and the concept of relationality has a short history of only decades. In light of this, it is no surprise that the word relate and its derivatives do not appear in Scripture.

Liam paused for a moment scanning his notes. In biblical days the idea of relatedness was defined as kinship, he continued. Even our idea of personhood was not known then as it is now. Aristotle was the first to observe the human person as a "thing amongst things," who could thus be reflected on as an entity in its environment. Humanity had to wait for Augustine and his *Confessions* for "the first great document in the history of introspective conscience," to be written.[73] The manner in which we see personhood today has taken shape over time. The study of humanity was known as anthropology only in the Middle Ages with the development of metaphysical psychology as an outflow of theology and philosophy. That connection began to change after the Enlightenment with the rise of the empirical in psychology and the natural and behavioural sciences. Concurrently, the idea of love evolved from a practical caring with the possibility of affection into the romantic notion so well known today. Liam said that he would have more to say about that further on.

The current recognition of the relational as being important helps us in developing our ideas about a God we know to be personal and thus relational. Liam explained that with everything existing in Christ the whole of creation is, what you might call, relationally wired. There was no time to get into the metaphysics of that but to say that even science is beginning to recognise that the relational can play a part in how our universe might function.

'But that's a different kind of relationality from what we have been talking about,' a student suggested.

'Spot on,' Liam agreed. 'There are levels of being in relation. At its most basic it is one entity responding to another. At its most advanced it concerns an intelligent being relating to the other, whereby the other may be lower on the creational scale like a person to a dog, or even to a tree. You may have heard of Martin Buber's I-Thou concept. In my presentation of the relational dynamics found in the Trinity I will focus mostly on the interaction between people.

The connection between the Trinity and human relating is found in the *imago dei* concept, people existing in the image of God. What this means has met with a variety of suggestions in theology through the ages. Two main ideas may be distinguished. The first one is the substantial/structural idea, meaning that humans have capabilities also found in God, such as the ability to reason and to be wilful. The other main idea is relational: that a fundamental and potential relationship between God and people exists. There is no reason to reject the idea that *imago dei* is both, is rational and relational.

Theologian Claus Westermann, in the footsteps of Karl Barth, holds that, "humans are created in such a way that their very existence is intended to be their relationship to God,"[74] Liam explained. Other modern theologians suggest that *imago dei* is the goal of humanity, which is a process that gradually evolves in history. Unsurprisingly, with the present emphasis on relationality in Western culture, theology has begun to consider *imago dei* as a social concept as well: believers in community, as the body of Christ. You can find this information more extensively in your lecture notes, he added.

There is one theologian I still would like to mention and then we will move on. Emil Brunner reasons that with *imago dei* the relational comes first followed by the other attributes in which people reflect God. "Only if he is loving, can he be truly man," Brunner states.[75] What Brunner means is that only by loving God will the full realisation of personhood become possible. This is to happen in communion with God, in community with other believers, while pursuing the mind of Christ. It seems, Liam suggested, that from Brunner's perspective only Christians can reach human relational potential in full. Anyone would like to make a comment on that?

'The Holy Spirit lives in us, so in that regard it would be true,' someone ventures.

'I know some non-Christians, who I like a lot better than some Christians,' said another.

'Isn't the point different though? We're talking here about the potential development of personhood, not its actuality,' a third person suggested.

Liam listened attentively as a few more comments were made.

The thing is, he said, that every person is relational

and carries the image of God, and not just the Christian. Relational dynamics are central to the development of personhood in general. Can Christians then develop further relationally than the non-believers? As far as it concerns an intended interaction with God obviously the answer is: yes. Brunner calls that a *full* development of personhood. I don't really like the choice of words, but okay. I suggest that those who do not believe in God are yet capable of developing relationally very well. You will know people like that, I hope. Perhaps that can be classified simply as *excellent* development of personhood. Whatever the case, there are primary relational principles involved that apply to everyone, I believe. They are relevant to any person and have outcomes regardless of religious association or even culture. Let's take a ten minutes break. Coffee and tea and other refreshments are on a table at the back of the room.

I mingled amongst the participants asking a few what had brought them to the lecture. One older person told me that she tried to do one short course per term, just to keep her mind active. That could be in anything that took her fancy. A youngish man was in the process of writing a thesis on relationality.

The lecture continued. From where does the human

spirit originate, Liam asked? From the inbreathing of God Genesis tells us.[76] God personally administered life which is a relational act. God is relational, what issues from God is relational, and thus our life is in essence relational. When the resurrected Jesus met his disciples for the first time after his death he breathed on them with the words, "Receive the Holy Spirit."[77] The human spirit born once, or born again, is relational. It can be said that relating is a spiritual activity. We are doing it all the time. If we are not interacting with others or nature, then we may be engaged in self-talk, that silent flow of thoughts regarding self-perception. In that we are relating to ourselves even though it may not really be consciously recognised. There is good and there is bad relating with subsequent outcomes. But how is the value of relating best decided on? What kind of relating fosters wellbeing and what doesn't? That question I will try to answer during these lectures. We need to reflect on where it all began, on divine reality.

We well know that God is love, which means ultimate relationality. From God issues our life. We carry the image of God and life shows us that our spirit is relational. I asked myself, where might I find the best information about good relating? The answer is rather obvious. I began to make a study of the relational dynamics within the Trinity not knowing what to expect, whether helpful insights would be found. The significance of my question made me suspect that our revelation about God would lead to some answers. I hoped for a way that would translate these insights into practicality; let the rubber hit the road. Ours is a practical God, who helps us get a grip on the important things in life. Relating sits at the top of the list. It became an exciting time of theological reflection and what I learned then, still excites me now. I practise it every day, as best I can, Liam said. Let's have a look at the Trinity.

The Three Persons exist *in relation* to each other. They affect each other. This involves a personal dynamic and thus they are *in relationship*. They will act relationally and that action is called *relationality*. So, what does divine relationality involve? How does God present in relational action? That is the question I raised, Liam said.

God *is* love, which translates into a primary relational principle. God will never act without love being its motivation. Love is the motivation between the Three Persons, and outwardly towards creation. Secondly, the complete unity between the Persons has been revealed to us. Please note that Trinity means not that the Three Persons become One Person. Rather, they are One God. They are One God because of the complete harmony and singleness of purpose between them. They are relationally One, and God because of their divinity. Unity is the second relational principle in the Trinity. So we have love and unity as primary relational principles. In human terms you may call these motivations. However, relationality is an action and the acting of God is the third principle. That acting concerns God's authority. The relational dynamics within the Trinity are: love, authority and unity.

'So that's why Jesus could become a human being and remain a member of the Trinity?' someone asked. 'He kept his divinity and though separated in Person, he was not relationally so.'

'Quite so,' Liam responded. 'And Jesus took that role because of the divine authority designated to him.'

Liam explained that each of the three Persons has a particular place and role in the relationship. Scripture is clear about the authority of each of the Three Persons. It must be stressed, he noted, that there is no pecking order, so to speak. That would be completely against the nature of love and unity. The Persons have no "egos" to defend and are completely unconcerned about their "position." Their concern is with the responsibility associated with each role and fulfilling that particular task to perfection.

When Apostle Paul writes that God has subjected all things under Christ's feet and that once Christ has realised that subjection within creation as a divine human being of free will, he himself will be subjected to his Father, it tells of the authorities of the Father and the Son[78]. When Jesus declares that the Spirit of truth will come, which occurred after his resurrection, who will guide into all truth and who will communicate in accordance with what Jesus seeks to convey, the authority of the Holy Spirit is partly explained. Jesus then tells his disciples that 'All that the Father has is mine; therefore I said that he (the Spirit) will take what is mine and declare it to you.'[79] Once again, this reveals the authority of each Person. Scripture defines these roles in other places, which I cannot discuss because of time restraints. Just look up the references in your notes.

Liam continued. We shall now have a look at the creation story and how the relational principles fit in with it. The different authorities within the Trinity are clearly revealed in how creation came about. The Father creates in the Son and by the Spirit. The Father is the source. The Son is the substance and the Spirit is the executive agent. When creation falls the Father sends the Son, in whom all holds together, to take responsibility as creation rests within his authority. The Son solves the problem and the Spirit upon word of the Father begins a new divine expression in the Son. In bringing new life the Spirit becomes personal to those who enter this New Creation. Finally, only the new will remain once the old has become obsolete.

In the creation story the three Trinitarian relational principles can be found. Roles and authorities are defined. Every action of God has love as its motivation. That cannot be otherwise. And, there is complete agreement and unity of purpose within God. All is expressed personally and thus relationally. God is never impersonal in creative expression. God never denies the divine nature. The three relational principles in the Trinity are love, authority and unity.

Liam suggested the participants should stand up for a minute and stretch their legs. He only had a few further comments to make in closing. After this break he turned his attention to the Adam and Eve story.

If Trinitarian relational dynamics are to be of value to human beings then that should show up from the beginning, in the Paradise story. Adam, the first human being, was given *authority* in having dominion over the earth. It meant the relational oversight of every animal and creature. They were named by him that is: personally known. Vegetation exclusively was to be the food for all. No creature killed another for sustenance or in anger. The lion grazed next to the lamb. However, in the naming Adam could not find a mate. Being a person of *love* he was looking for reciprocity in kind for his love to become truly meaningful. God understood and presented him with Eve. The ultimate expression of love in creation, between beings in the image of God, now had been established. They became *one* flesh. Creation was complete and God rested. This rest signifies that the creation existed in accordance with the nature of God; it was unified, cared for and at peace with itself, all fitting in its rightful place. Love, authority and unity were active without restriction.

We know what happened next, Liam said. It will be the topic in a fortnight's time, plus how the Trinitarian principles can work for us.

I didn't catch up with him after the lecture as a number of participants sought him out. Outside, it had begun to rain.

11

The Trinitarian relational model and wellbeing;
Relating and the mind of Christ

SOMETIMES THE MIND is effortlessly calm and also reflective, engaged in its own dynamics of remembrance. All is still within me and the night silent. The lake keeps on shimmering and has not a breeze upon it. My body feels relaxed without a tremor of restlessness. I think of Liam and miss him much. In that second lecture he explained what gave him more pleasure than anything else academic. How love might become practical for anyone, regardless of colour, creed or education.

Upon arrival, I noticed that attendance that evening had increased. The lectures were being recorded so catching up on what had been missed was easy. At the start Liam put on a devil's mask that he once brought home from Bali. It was to remind himself that Satan was alive and well. I think he kept it in a closet at the college. He briefly looked around and got the expected laugh. Liam could be funny on occasions. In taking the mask off he growled that it was not a laughing matter, the devil and sin, and smiled disarmingly. We were ready for the next instalment in discovering the nature and importance of relating.

Last time, we concluded with a mention of God's rest and the peacefulness of creation. The word that describes it best is shalom. The resurrected Jesus spoke the word as a first greeting to his disciples.[80] The future promises that to us. One day all will be shalom. Presently, the world is anything but shalom because of Adam and Eve violating God's relational principles as is explained in Genesis. Eve broke the *love* bond with God through disobedience and invited Adam to eat of the forbidden fruit as well. Adam damaged his God-given *authority* by being irresponsible and complying with Eve's suggestion. The *unity* of purpose that existed between God and people was destroyed. The relational power of sin entered the world. Life was destined to die in future and creatures began to devour each other instead of eating vegetation. Humans became conscious of both the powers of good *and* evil struggling within them and are, as far as we can tell, the only creatures to have this choice as a wilful intention.

The security of an open relational bond with God

became a sense of dread, a psycho-spiritual uncertainty for Adam and Eve. Having dominion now meant working by the sweat of the brow to make a living and when that was neglected scarcity would certainly come. Adam and Eve felt invaded into in their own person, vulnerable and subject to disintegration. Their unity of identity had been destroyed. Instead of living solely under God's relational dynamics of Love, Authority and Unity, they were now *dictated* to by sin and *deserted* by creation for a secure supply of their basic needs. They experienced a vulnerability within themselves as well as towards their environment. They lived in *disharmony* with all and were in danger of their lives because of predators. The power of sin, a destructive force, began to rule against the power of God power, against love. Both love and sin are relational. The world had entered a different relational state. The relational dynamics of sin, opposed to love are, Dictatorship, Desertion and Disharmony.

The horrific consequences of this change became very clear in the next generation, Liam explained. The story of Cain and Abel typifies the right and wrong relational dynamics. Cain did not seek to relate to God correctly. But he was offered acceptance by God, if he would change his ways. Unity of purpose in harmony with God could be restored. Note an important point, Liam stressed: God considered Cain, born in a sinful state, capable of making this choice for the good against the temptations of sin. If successful, blessings would follow. Cain had a choice. It means that relationally people are able of change towards the positive and one day they will be held accountable for that by God, Liam suggested. Cain preferred *disharmony* with God, and with his brother, which resulted into the ultimate act of *dictatorship*. Cain murdered Abel. When God inquired with Cain about Abel, he *deserted* his brother completely with the response: "Am I my brother's keeper?" The three destructive relational dynamics resulting from sin had become well and truly established within creation. Little wonder that Jesus and the Apostles kept encouraging towards the relationally positive. *Love* one another is the thrust of the whole Bible. May they be at *one*, Jesus prayed fervently in his High Priestly Prayer.[81] Take the right *authority* over your life, live responsibly in the light of God's law, is the continual advice. These three Trinitarian principles will bring the wellbeing life deserves. The negative principles reflecting sin, of dictatorship, desertion and disharmony, will set us on the road to disintegration.

Liam took a sip of water and for a moment gazed out of the window in silence. All was dark outside so he must have mostly seen the lecture room reflected in the glass.

Nobody interrupted the drifting of his mind. It would have been sort of improper. After a while he continued with combining positive and negative within personhood.

The thing is, Liam said, that these six relational dynamics, three for good and three for evil, play out within each of us without escape. They are part of the make-up of a human being. Consider that people are fundamentally relational and you will understand how important it is for us to get a proper handle on how these dynamics work. What we might do about that. The psychological and behavioural consequences. They must be addressed.

Relating is a psycho-spiritual activity that issues from the human spirit. Central to the nature of the spirit is what we call disposition or attitude. A composite expression of various factors. It is shaped by personality, ability, culture, education and experience. Experience is a significant determinant in our relational responses based on how we have been related to over the years. That begins immediately after birth, or as some would suggest already in the womb, and continues throughout life. These relational experiences leave, what may be called, a relational imprint, a relational memory bank, which is not static but produces outcomes. Every person carries that within and has to deal with the consequences. If this imprint is excessively negative, life looks like trouble. A good imprint facilitates the possibilities of personal wellbeing. Wellbeing will not be automatic. But when the relational imprint is good, it can be achieved. Psychiatrist Eric Fromm consciously linked mental health to the task of "achieving the aims of human life," which in his estimation entails independence, integrity and the ability to love.[82] That aligns with my suggestion of aiming for correctly used authority, unity of purpose and love. Fromm is the author of a once popular book called *The Art of Loving*, which is relationally focused rather than sexually.

'Any questions?' Liam asked.

A moment of silence filled the room.

'You are suggesting that who we are, is much determined by relational experience?' someone queried.

'Yes. What has most affected us in our lives? I bet it's always relationally based for either good or not so.'

'You will show us how to understand that better and to deal with it?' another asked.

'To a point, yes,' Liam confirmed.

He followed on in stating that the model he would present reflects the advancement of the behavioural sciences and the empirical findings of psychology in particular. A number of professionals in this field are familiar with the model's content and find no fault with it. A retired professor in psychology, who used to be a colleague of Liam's, had scrutinized Liam's ideas and found them acceptable.[83] Due mainly to the fact that the categories used in the model are easily understood. The comments made are readily confirmed by common sense, and the overall information is general rather than academic. What we will discuss is *not* a tool by which to diagnose and treat deep-seated psychological problems, Liam made clear. Such problems may well be the outcome of bad relational interaction over the years. They may be understood in their origin from insights on Trinitarian relating, but finding a solution is the task of the professional psychologist. It is recommended to seek out such a person when the need is obvious.

It was time for a break and, in my case, a cup of tea.

Before we look at the relational categories, I would like to make a comment about the word love, Liam continued, once everyone was seated again. When we say God is love, the word love carries a primary value. However, when I use it as a category of relating that is no longer so, it has become an aspect of relational dynamic. It must be understood that love, authority and unity all are an expression of love as primary. Likewise, dictatorship, desertion and disharmony are an expression of sin. Furthermore, though we will dissect relational dynamics using these six categories, three positive and negative, it must be understood that the relating itself always is *one* action. What that action is like, is determined by which of the categories gain the upper hand. We can personally control that to a degree. A model is a handy way in which to present insights and doing so in a manner that will be practical.

A full outline of the Trinitarian relational model is found in the back of your notes (see Appendix). You will find that each of the six relational categories is explained using seven specific factors. Today I will concentrate on the first two and the last of those factors. They are most descriptive of the dynamics involved for each category. If you study the model carefully, you will have no problem in figuring out how the other four factors are relevant in how relating works. I will not get that far today, Liam said.

The first factor is called *Fundamental Orientation*. It is the root cause of a relational expression and corresponds with the six principal categories. The second factor concerns the *Primary Expression* of a category. This is an action word indicating the nature of a communication. Actually, it is the word most to remember when relating. *Fundamental Orientation* and *Primary Expression* are the two sides of the one coin, so to speak.

The last of the seven factors is the *Primary Outcome* of a relational category – a most important factor to keep in mind. It gives the potential psycho-spiritual consequence of a relational category, when a person is consistently exposed to it. It is the long-term effect of a relational expression. It alludes to the relational imprint of a person and probable relational tendencies.

Liam brought up a PowerPoint slide explaining that he had called the three positive relational categories *Motivators* and the three negative ones *Demoralisers*.

Orientation/Expression   **Outcome**

Motivators

Love/Care	**Compassion**
Authority/Responsibility	**Freedom**
Unity/Integrity	**Wholeness**

Demoralisers

Dictatorship/Oppression	**Rebellion**
Desertion/Neglect	**Anarchy**
Disharmony/Manipulation	**Weakness**

Love is a complex emotion. But we all know what it means *to care*. We can do it, when we decide to, Liam said. What we may not realise is, that by exposing someone consistently to good caring enables that person to care also, to become *compassionate*. I am speaking here about relational exposure from birth onwards. I will explain all the categories from that perspective.

The flipside of Authority is *being responsible*. The word authority has negative overtones these days, but that should not concern us. Authority tells us to drive on the left side of the road. That avoids accidents and is helpful. I must then be a responsible citizen and adhere to that. It is best for me and others. Doing so gives me *freedom* to travel where I wish. Authority sets sensible boundaries and takes responsibility for those to be obeyed. It teaches another person to operate within healthy restrictions and thus to remain free.

The third motivator of Unity encourages us to have *integrity*. We must be people who can be trusted. A person of integrity is dependable and consistent. That helps others to become an integrated person by not continually being exposed to behavioural uncertainties. Growing up surrounded by integrity fosters *wholeness* of being.

Liam asked whether there were questions.

'But what if I don't grow up in that kind of ideal environment?'

'Nobody grows up in a perfect family,' Liam agreed. 'The relational mix over time makes a relational imprint on a person. If this mix is reasonably positive, we should be okay. If not, we will have problems. In many cases the imprint is good enough to help us function as relationally decent people. But we must always try to improve on that.'

'How about, when it's bad? Are we then hopelessly lost?' another asked.

'Not lost, I believe,' Liam said. 'But it is a problem and it will be tough on the person concerned. Undoing the negative effects of behavioural exposure needs a focused response. I'll make a few comments about that later. Let's first look at the negative side in detail.'

Dictatorship involves *oppression*, an environment in which you do as you are told. It can become violent, but need not be. You will experience a lack of true care and will feel angry about that. That anger translates into *rebellion*, the urge to kick out against family and society. Also, you will be angry with yourself. Much of what is expressed outwardly is usually first experienced inwardly. You will blame yourself for your incapacity to cope.

Another damaging relational dynamic is Desertion, when you are exposed to *neglect*. That also makes you angry over time. If they don't take responsibility for me, why should I be responsible, is the line of thought. Away with responsibility, let's have *anarchy* and become out of control. You will notice that each category produces outcomes in accordance with its own kind. Of course, things are never as clear cut as the six categories suggest, Liam reiterated. There will be a mix of exposure.

Finally, let's look at the most subtle of the categories: Disharmony. It is expressed by *manipulation*. Manipulation is so easily done and so destructive long-term. Hey, I dig you man, would you mind doing me a favour? That sounds great, but is in fact manipulative. Manipulation is relational blackmail. It seeks to subject you to someone's wishes by making personal acceptance conditional. It undermines self-determination. When growing up in a manipulative environment, it robs you of a mind of your own, which results in the disintegration of personhood and *weakness*. All of this is demoralising. The influences of sin in our lives can be relationally very destructive.

Liam suggested we stretch our legs for a moment.

I have found the easiest way to remember what I am about relationally is asking three questions, he continued, and showed a slide on the screen. These questions are simple but attitudinally important.

Do I?
1. **Care** or **Oppress**
2. act **Responsibly** or practise **Neglect**
3. have **Integrity** or **Manipulate**

I always ask myself this and my wife knows about it. She tries to catch me out when I phrase a request or make a comment manipulatively. I don't seem to care too badly overall, but I have made mistakes. I regret that and pressures can catch you out. Responsibility may be a problem, occasionally. I feel that I can be reasonably trusted and my integrity is okay. I'm not perfect and do not expect that of myself. I consider myself relationally adequate and work on keeping it that way.

Ask yourself the questions on the screen and you will be on the right track. You must remember that there is never a vacuum in your relational engagements. These factors will always be active. You are to decide which ones will have prominence and act on that. If not the factors will decide it for you naturally. It brings me to an earlier question asked, about what your chances are when growing up in relational circumstances that are not supportive.

The Trinitarian relational model will not solve bad situations. It does show a way forward. The model works best for those who are reasonably proficient in relating okay. They will understand relating better in using the model and can function relationally with good success. If that is achieved by you, I will be a happy man. In our society where good information is often classified as interesting and soon discarded for the next interesting topic, I despair sometimes. Why neglect in giving helpful information a real go? I hope you will try this model out. Those in your care, and also you yourself, will really benefit from it.

When things are bad and you have been relationally mistreated, your option is to learn the ways of positive relating and try hard to manage those. The positive will overcome the negative over time, when consistently applied. I have few illusions about the struggle that involves. For Christians the help and healing of the Holy Spirit is a distinct advantage. One thing, we should all be attentive to, is our self-talk. It reveals much about who we really are. Insist on making it positive. Care for yourself. Take responsibility for yourself. Don't tell yourself white lies or real ones. With those lies you are manipulating your own soul.

Liam reflected for a moment. I would like to say, that I have taken an interpersonal approach in my explanation. The idea for designing the model arose from a desire to help parents evaluate common attitudes and interactions between themselves and their children. I was presenting a series on stages of personal development from birth onward and found the relational aspect lacking. That was years ago. Of course, the effects of relating are much broader than family life. The principles apply in business, society as a whole and in our attitude to the environment. Get relating right and the good life will follow. Get it wrong and people or nature will suffer.

For us Christians there is a particular point I wish

to make. It concerns spirituality and relationality, which over time I have come to see as one and the same. There are many definitions of spirituality actually, each a little different from the other. For me, everyone is a spiritual person and expresses spirituality. That spirituality is relational and it can be positive or negative. When as a Christian I am encouraged to love God and to express the nature and mind of Christ, it requires little more than consistently applying the Trinitarian relational principles in life - towards God, others and nature. Get that right and the Lord will be pleased. These principles come from God and reflect God. It is the way in which we may be sure to love our neighbour as ourselves. I dare say that when a non-Christian lives by the relational principles, God will be equally pleased. God loves all of creation regardless of sin. Knowing Christ personally is a privilege and let's make sure we live up to that. Not perfectly but good enough. Be relationally positive, take the principles to heart and you need not worry any longer whether you might represent Christ sufficiently. In a world that has become very scientific but relationally focused, God remains ever relevant. Knowledge of God's principles helps in gaining an understanding of creation and how it functions.

It's time for bed at the foot of Big Red. A wind is rippling the lake and the night now chilly. Jake has been fast asleep for a while. Tomorrow we will be back in civilization – to a point. I am not sure how I feel about that.

12

Interpretive categories of experience and the relational

WHEN JAKE AND I walk into Australia's most iconic bush pub on a Saturday morning a surprise awaits us. A plane load of Sydney-siders smartly dressed in their outback city clothes fills the main bar enjoying drinks before lunch. It presents a feast of fashion, taste and vocal noise. Had I been on my own, I would have settled in a corner and watch this pop-in crowd with interest. Groups of people can be fascinating. As it is, we make our way into the side bar, which is virtually deserted. Later that afternoon a large prop plane takes off from the airfield behind the pub towards another destination of expensive outback tourism, no doubt: Uluru perhaps, for dinner and an overnight stay. In Birdsville, central Australia, you are not isolated from the large coastal cities. It attracts tourists from all over the world. After more than a week in the silent and remote bush, that city bustle in the bar grinds on me.

This morning we had taken our time packing up at Big Red. The lake's water level was low enough to make a crossing quite near to our campsite and the 20 miles over dirt road to Birdsville, a town of about 100 inhabitants, was quickly covered. A visit to the cemetery revealed a little of the history of the place. Just out of town on a slight hill graves are grouped together in different places. People died young in those early days.

Since 1882 horse races have been held in Birdsville on a sandy track. The event still happens the first week of September every year. That weekend the town population increases to 6000. Professionally trained horses run the main race for considerable prize money these days. Access to the town is by air or dirt roads winding seemingly forever through barren country. A few years ago the race had to be cancelled due to continual heavy rains. It made the roads impassable. That happens only occasionally.

Upon arrival in the town Jake and I had bought a pie at the bakery across from the pub, filled the car's tank and our jerry cans up with diesel and booked into the caravan park. We pitched our tent down the hill next to the local lagoon and adjacent to a tree for some shade. It was time for our first shower in days, a welcome experience. I told Jake not to leave anything small unattended as black crows would carry it away. These birds are a nuisance and can be noisy when they talk to each other loudly over a distance. Refreshed and invigorated we walked towards the Birdsville Hotel, the place many Australians would like to visit at least once. Our national psyche is interesting like that. Most of us live in the cities, but the call of the outback is strong, at least so we are to believe. In my case, that is undoubtedly correct.

The Birdsville Hotel is a sturdy rectangular white-washed building of stone with small brown timber windows and a veranda all round. The walls extend a little above the veranda showing a horizontal line of brown brick against the white and hiding the guttering of the metal clad pitched roof. Instead of lattice the veranda features short white strips of timber rounded at the bottom end. These are nailed vertically next to each other along the veranda's full length. At the street corner, where the walls take a 45 degree angles for a short distance, the hotel shows a small gable that proudly reads: Established 1884. It is a typical Australian bush building in a place where suffocating temperatures may be expected every year. The tar of the bitumen main road, that runs the length of the town, is known to melt in those hot days.

Birdsville, near the Queensland and South Australia border, used to be a very busy town when border crossing custom duties were payable. But that was years ago. Now it is mostly a central stopover for outback travellers, a tourist destination, and a pick-up point of supplies for a few cattle stations. No place is quite like Birdsville. Wherever you stand, you can see the edge of town in the knowledge that beyond it are miles of nothing but bush country.

Like all iconic pubs in Australia the walls inside are hung with paraphernalia and history. This old-time look disguises the great efficiency of this building that can cater for a large group of people. Jake and I order a beer at the side bar and make for a table near one of the windows. The idea is to waste our time pleasantly for a day and travel on tomorrow for a long stretch. It will be two nights yet before I will drop Jake off at the terminal in Port Augusta for the bus to Adelaide. He asks me how much more to go with our discussions. I tell him the end is in sight, but it will need today and tomorrow. We decide to talk a little while enjoying these beers and then continue after our evening meal, which will be at this pub. Jake looks a picture of health. The fresh air in the bush has done him good. He has the energy of a young person and a mind that does not quickly tire. We spend some time reflecting on our trip before continuing with the thoughts of Liam.

'We'll discuss a little bit of philosophy,' I tell him. 'Ideas about interpretive experience. It won't take long.'

Jake smiles. Philosophy is his interest.

'Relational encounters involve both perception and assessment', I begin. 'I perceives what the other is like and evaluates from experience how to interpret that. That other may be anything. It can be a person, an animal or whatever. The relational possibilities detected during the confrontation will vary. They may be neutral, encouraging or discouraging. Whatever the case, the other is perceived in three aspects that together present the one identity of that other.'

I sip some beer.

'Three aspects? Perhaps category is a better word.' Jake is showing his education.

'Yes. Liam was rather pleased about the idea and we'll see why. The categories of interpretation of the other are: its nature, its authority and its coherence. Beyond that, the object of attention cannot be known, while the extent to which it is known depends on interpretive ability. That applies to the known world and the unseen one. In the spiritual world it concerns responses to what is being perceived supernaturally.'

'Go on,' Jake says.

'When confronted with an animal, I can classify the creature as such for it has the nature of an animal. Also, it has the authority of an animal, which means it behaves like one. Furthermore, it holds together, it looks like an animal.'

Jake thinks this over and nods his head.

'I may recognise the animal as a horse by the same principles. If it is indeed a horse, it will have the nature of one, it will behave like one, and it holds together and looks like one. My experience tells me in observing these three aspects of the animal, that I am confronted with a horse.'

'And that can be specialised further,' Jake suggests. 'When I'm confronted with a race horse, I will detect that by its competitive nature, its alert behaviour and its build; that kind of thing.'

'Yes. Change one of those markers and you have a different kind of horse.' As always, Jake is quick in the uptake.

'The same counts for a stone,' I continue. 'I know a stone by its nature, which is hard, heavy and lifeless. It has an authority that indicates "I'm not moving of my own account." And finally, it has the coherence of a stone.'

'Okay,' Jake says. 'Nature, authority and coherence, those are the three categories whereby I make sense of my environment. That is interesting.'

'Perhaps you don't make sense of it,' I reply. 'You may be unfamiliar with interpreting the characteristics of a certain manifestation. You are unable to, or cannot fully decide on, classifying what you are confronted with. More will need to be discovered about it first. The discovery though will follow the pattern of nature, authority and coherence in shaping an understanding.'

'Would you like another beer?' Jake is looking at his empty glass. That would be nice. While he walks to the bar I gaze through the window onto a dusty road. A dirty utility passes by, rugged and well worn, with large spotlights on the bullbar and a swivel light on top for night shooting. Only the hardy are suited to this kind of country and have opened it up, both men and women. I have come to respect that greatly. Jake returns with our beers.

'As I mentioned,' I explain, picking up the cold frosty glass of amber liquid, 'the divine realm is detected and interpreted in the same manner.'

'You mean, God?' Jake queries.

'I mean everything that transcends our world. The gods and spirits, or nothingness for that matter, all enter human cognition by the categories of: What is it like? What can it do? How does it hold together?'

Jake waits for an illustration. I give it some thought.

'Take the Buddhist example of nothingness, for instance. It may be suggested that the nature of it, is being empty of all creation. It invites to a complete escape from reality as it is generally known - that is what it can do. And, it holds together as "nothing" against our objective reality.'

'I don't know much about Buddhism,' Jake admits.

'The idea of "the gods" in general is determined similarly,' I continue. 'The question always is: What they are like? What can they do? And, how is the divine structure maintained, what classifies them as gods? The Christian God fits these categories as well, regardless of whether you are a believer or not.'

'You mean that for my idea about God to make sense it must include these three categories, even though I may be an atheist?' Jake suggests.

'Yes. Perhaps you have the right idea about God. But, you stand in relation to that idea without it reaching the level of interaction. God remains just an idea. You may perhaps have the wrong idea about God. It makes no difference. You have still arrived at the idea by the interpretive categories we are discussing.'

'And if I don't interact with the idea, you still call that relational?' Jake wonders.

'Technically, all ideas are relational, because I take a stance towards them. I can accept them, reject them, remain neutral, avoid or ignore them. That response is relational.'

'Fair enough,' Jake concedes. 'But why did dad take a fancy to this?'

Why indeed? I tell Jake I must visit the amenities and will be back shortly. He is comfortable in this outback pub enjoying it. Upon my return to the bar I find him at one of the walls perusing old photos and leave him to it. Both of us are relaxed, with an afternoon to spare. The old pub has an interesting history.

'Liam saw a correlation between how we make sense of our world and how God is known to us,' I tell Jake a little later. 'Obvious, of course, for the idea of God fits into us experiencing our world. As such, the divine is not known apart from the interpretive categories. For the Christian, it means that essentially God is love by nature, has complete authority and is One God, who is a Trinity.'

Jake nods

'The interpretive categories are relational. It led Liam to an interesting question. He asked next, whether our experience being translated into our understanding by these categories might apply to understanding the relational itself. Can the relational be explained using the three categories? Furthermore, might that explanation be linked to relationality within the Trinity? That makes sense, because the relational originates with God. Thirdly, if relevant to us as people, how can such an explanation of the relational become practical?'

'And he found that it could,' Jake surmised. Why otherwise would his father have been enthused with the idea?

'Yes, he did. He was able to use the categories of nature, authority and coherence in explaining what relationality is about. That will be our topic for tonight.'

We walk through the town past the specially equipped truck that brings broken down cars back from the desert and visit the Old Birdsville Courthouse. Back at our tent, just sitting by the lagoon for an hour looking around is a soothing experience. I find that in the bush everything slows down and I can spend hours doing nothing. At home that simply is unimaginable.

When the sun begins to approach the horizon Jake and I are back at the pub for an excellent steak dinner. It is then that I tell him about the Trinitarian Relational Model and sketch out the gist of it on some paper. Jake doesn't say much. His mind is only partly on the information and it matters not. In the end I reiterate my earlier promise to mail him the full outline of the model once back home. Our dinner in that old pub at a worn timber table is a special time. We have become friends. I will never forget that evening in outback Birdsville.

13

Love's Day in Court

WE LEFT BIRDSVILLE early in the morning. That was yesterday. Presently, I am driving south of Port Augusta where I dropped Jake off at the bus terminal with time to spare. The main shopping street close to the terminal is nothing special, but a place to stretch your legs after a long drive. I suggested this to Jake when we said our farewells. Handing him his rucksack I found a big smile on his face. Neither of us is good at goodbyes. That much became clear. But we understood each other perfectly.

Driving on bitumen is a pleasure after miles of tracks and corrugated roads. We had hit the tarmac at Lyndhurst today some 200 miles away and pumped up the tires to 40 psi. That is hours ago now. Soon I will turn off this Adelaide bound highway east towards Wilmington. It is in the direction of Sydney, which you can reach after a few days travelling. My destination is less than an hour south of Wilmington, where Liv and I own a shack in the Southern Flinders. In my spare time I work at developing that property. It will be my bed for tonight, my real bed.

The Birdsville track, which took us yesterday all the way to Maree, has a mystique about it; the kind of road you need to travel if ever you have a chance. It offers you unspoken bragging rights, or so it seems. In the early days of colonization it was a stock route. Perhaps that is the reason for its attraction, its fame living on in Australian folklore. For me, I won't complain if I never see it again. The wide dirt road, over which many a semitrailer finds its way, makes for anything but a pleasant drive. You have to keep your eyes constantly focused on what might be the best line of travel. Where the fewest potholes can be found and the least corrugation; how to minimize the potential damage to your car. Speeds of 50 miles per hour are quite possible, but care is necessary. Extra care when the road has not recently been graded. The Birdsville Track progresses through the uninspiring landscape of the Sturt Stony Desert.

The best moment of that drive came while having an early lunch at the lowly slung pub at Mungerannie. It has fuel and a campsite, neither of which we needed. The Australian behind the bar explained that actually he lives in Canada and is doing very well financially. He visits his old friend the pub owner for a few months every year to help with renovations during the quiet times. Those times reach into summer with temperatures so high that metal work is almost impossible. They start building at sunrise for some hours and again before sunset. Even then it would be hot. I wondered about living that far away in the middle of nowhere, with few for company and being pleased with it. Each to his own and you cannot but admire them.

Jake and I arrived in the small town of Maree eventually and on a better dirt road made it to Farina for the night. To its campsite near the creek. Farina is a ghost town. Once a bustling place of hundreds of inhabitants where the camel trains stopped over, it now shows interesting historic ruins. At dusk we took a walk amongst those for an hour. The optimism of people in where they could settle successfully in the outback is amazing. Farina is but one example of many. A group of volunteers is trying to open up the bakery again a few days each year at Easter when many off-road enthusiasts pass by.

The Wilmington turnoff is in sight. It warns me to keep my mind on the driving. I take the left turn slowly. The road soon winds through a pass in the Flinders Ranges.

About half an hour south of Wilmington is the town of Melrose. It is quite a pleasant place at the foot of Mount Remarkable. Popular with hikers and mountain bikers. Melrose is the first group of dwelling in the Flinders to gain town status in 1853. In South Australian context, it thus has a long history. Since Wilmington, I have driven through farm country, mostly crops with a few sheep to supplement the farmer's income. There are fields to the east as far as the eye can see with a low mountain range close by to the west. That range flattens out further on and allows for farming all the way to the outskirts of Adelaide 130 miles away. In a good year the quantity of crop produced in South Australia is enormous and a welcome boost to the economy.

I stop at the old smithy for a welcome coffee. This small ramshackle building features an obsolete workshop at the street front with fire place, large bellow complete with pulley, anvil and a water basin for cooling the red hot metal. All the tools needed by a smith are on display plus a great number of implements used in farming many years ago. The building consisting of timber, stone and sheet metal clearly shows the ingenuity of bush carpentry of the past. Some inner walls are simply clad with hessian. I take my coffee into the enclosed courtyard at the back and sit down on an old chair next to a vintage millstone.

My thoughts drift back to the trip and to Jake my

companion. He has the mind of his father and the even temperament of his mum. I decide to call Sandy tomorrow to touch base. Jake has already done so from the bus station. Sandy will be picking him up in Adelaide. My old mate Liam enters my thoughts with sadness. Having spent time with his son sharpened the loss.

On a down day, Liam could be despondent. He was a sensitive man who took the mess in our world to heart and that depressed him. At those moments, which happened not often, he wondered whether seeing the history of our universe as a divine love story was simply an illusion. But he found accepting that thought impossible. We haven't seen the end yet, Baz, he would say. All the pain and grief in the world makes no sense, unless you believe in the end game. He sounded both slightly desperate and utterly convinced. You have to look at life from that perspective, he insisted. And I don't blame anyone, if they don't manage it. Most don't even know about it. They don't know what Jesus achieved and those who do, may not take it seriously. Or will not fully understand it. Yesterday I read a poem by St. John of the Cross about a young lone shepherd boy whose love is discarded.

Since our lunch in McLaren Vale, he had bought a copy of the complete works of St. John. He grabbed the

book from the shelf and began flicking through the
pages. I love John of the Cross and knew what Liam
was looking for. After a while he found it. In typical
Liam fashion he read it through reflectively first. Listen
to this, the second stanza:

> He weeps, but not from the wound of love,
> there is no pain in such affliction,
> even though the heart is pierced;
> he weeps in knowing he's been forgotten.[84]

Doesn't that depress you? Liam asked.

I could see his point and wondered whether
reading these lines had become the catalyst for his
sombre mood to set in. I know the poem well. John is
one of the greatest poets Spain has ever produced. I tell
you, Baz, Liam announced: love will have its day in
court! He gently closed the pages shut. I was certain that
tomorrow would be a much better day for him. It
usually was, after these occasional bouts of melancholic
musing.

Love's day in court was the topic Jake and I had
discussed around our last campfire at Farina. It
completes Liam's thoughts on a theology of love. The
central factors in divine love confronting our world at
the end of time are, unsurprisingly: the nature of love,

relationality, and the ability of choice. Liam preferred the word choice above free will, for he found it to represent more accurately what love's questions will be about. Before attending to those questions it needed to be understood that the human disposition of sin has been dealt with by Jesus on the cross and will not be held against anyone. Likewise, the creation will not be blamed for the war of destruction that sin wages within it. What will be called to notice are the wilful relational choices made by people for either good or evil. The standard by which to measure it is the Trinitarian relational principles.

In a court of love the benchmark is love. Not only with regard to the accused, but first of all for the court itself; it will have to dispense justice in love. Love seeks to embrace, to forgive and to restore. But it will call a spade a spade. It seeks to forgive, but it will not overlook. No-one is expected to be perfect, far from. Love does not have a pointing finger, rather open arms of acceptance. Mistakes are soon covered by love where possible. Liam held that there would not be a checklist of individual deeds, so to speak – more an overall picture of the nature of a person's life in light of what the world has thrown at that person. God will be gracious.

In the court of divine love there are two types of cases before it. Those concerned with followers of Jesus and those of people who are not. Scripture is quite clear on that, even though often this information remains little discussed. For instance, I have never heard anyone preach a sermon on the topic: the judgment seat of Christ. It seems overly negative within the framework of a positive Gospel. But Jesus and Paul made some clear comments on God's judgments - about this court of love.

Every believer will be facing an account of personal behaviour before the judgment seat of Christ – the good as well as the bad.[85] This evaluation does not involve the question of eternal life as that has been settled. Rather, a Christian's works will become manifest and tested as if through fire – the purifying gaze of love. Rewards await those whose works withstand that scrutiny and loss for those whose works don't. The latter will enter their heavenly future, but as if through fire.[86] The nature of God is to reward rather than destroy. Only when the demands of love have been greatly violated will the experience of loss occur. When genuinely accepting Jesus as the Lord of one's life all wrongdoing is forgiven, the slate of sin is wiped clean. The task is to keep it that way, to live a relationally good life. When making a mistake, you own up and ask for forgiveness. It keeps the slate clean. Apply the Lord's Prayer[87] daily to how you live and all is well. Make sure to practise the Trinitarian relational principles towards God and the world. Be a person who cares; who takes responsibility and who can be trusted – who is an open book before God. With the slate of sin clean and your good acts duly recorded by the Lord, you can live life looking forward to meeting him in person.

Apart from those who will receive rewards and those who suffer loss, there is a third kind of person in the Christian camp. Those, who declare allegiance to Christ falsely. They will proclaim to have done mighty works in the name of Jesus, but he said not to know of them with the stern words, "depart from me you evildoers."[88] God appears to have honoured a calling on the name of Jesus with miracles, but will not accept the hypocrites involved. Love will not be fooled. Dark hearts will not prevail in the Kingdom of Heaven.

That leaves those who have not followed Christ. How will love deal with this sea of humanity? The criteria of assessment are the knowledge of good and evil and the choices wilfully made. Those choices are relational ones and thus the Trinitarian principles apply. While on earth Jesus explained to his disciples that the hour will come when all the dead shall rise in response to his command. Then they will come, Jesus said, "those who have done good, to the resurrection of life, and those who have done evil, to the resurrection of judgment."[89] It is clear that behaviour is being judged here by the qualifying standard of good and evil – of love and sin. Apostle Paul refers to this event suggesting that a person's conscience will either accuse or excuse them, when God judges the secrets of people by Jesus Christ.[90] Jesus presented a similar idea when foretelling the gathering of the nations that are to face him. [91] He told many people, "you have done well" and they wondered how. You decided to *care* was the response. "You fed the hungry, gave drink to the thirsty." Others he told that they had disqualified themselves by their callous behaviour. They said they had never met him. "So you thought," the Lord replied. "But I was there, and you did not care!" Get away from me.

Love will have its day in court and will be just. Its questions will be put to people old enough to express care purposefully, to be held justifiably responsible for their actions, and from whom integrity may be expected. That disqualifies the young, who may enter into love's embrace without such scrutiny. Every person will be faced with the door named Jesus Christ. Multitudes will pass through, but some won't make it.

It raises the notion of hell. Modern thought suggests that the concept as understood today became popular due to Dante's *Inferno*.[92] It misrepresents the idea of Hades Jesus referred to. Liam figured it to be a place where relationality is altogether void of love and fully dictated by sin. Those who are so corrupted that love cannot find sufficient connection are destined for it, he surmised. Only God really knows. It will be far fewer in number than is often suggested.

It's much better to focus on the positive Baz, Liam would say. Just imagine: what nobody has ever seen or heard, or even imagined in their wildest dreams, that's what the Lord has ready waiting for those who love him.[93] It will be phenomenally fantastic. Life can be difficult and leaving this world, for many of us, will mean liberation. You cannot really understand God's love, Baz, unless you include the endgame. You must include the endgame!

Thus spoke Liam, my best friend and loving theologian.

My coffee cup has been empty for a while. Better move on for the half hour drive to the 100 years old little church with its nine stained glass windows - just beautiful - which is our shack.

Thank you!
You have finished the main story. Part 2 presents the full version of the Trinitarian Relational Model

PART TWO

The Trinitarian Relational Model

Trinitarian Relating

Relating in accordance with the Trinity involves three primary dynamics that are *positive*. They foster wellbeing and better so when intentionally applied. Three *negative* dynamics are operative as well and to be avoided. They cause disintegration.

These six dynamics are fundamental to personhood. They are inevitably expressed as one in relational interaction. In this, the dynamics most in sync with the disposition of a person will have prominence in shaping the nature of the interaction.

Each primary dynamic can be explained using seven factors – the first being its *Fundamental Orientation* and the last the *Primary Outcome*. There are five intermediate steps.

The seven factors that shape a primary dynamic.

1. *Fundamental Orientation*
It is the root cause of a relational expression and is reflected in the primary word given for it.

2. *Primary Expression*

It indicates how the Fundamental Orientation is communicated. It is an action word.

3. *Technique*

It involves the method by which the Primary Expression is realised and the environment thus created.

4. *Relational Interaction*

It expresses the intent of a communication – the principle message the other will receive. It is Technique translated into a projection that is experienced.

5. *Basic Attitude*

It defines the relational nature of a person. It directly connects with Primary Expression and Technique. Basic Attitude is a central category.

6. *Existential Reality*

It describes what kind of place is available to the recipient of a communication. How it affects the person on the 'inside'. It is shaped by all the other factors together and determines the Primary Outcome.

7. *Primary Outcome*

It is the potential psycho-spiritual outcome of a relational dynamic when being consistently exposed to it. Primary Outcome is the long-term effect of a relational expression and leaves an imprint.

(The model in full is presented further on)

Positive Relating

The three positive dynamics of Trinitarian relating are called *Motivators.* A Motivator's nature is expressed as *Fundamental Orientation/Primary Expression.*

MOTIVATOR 1 *Love/Care*

Expressing love in everyday relating is not just a feeling but an intention of care. It can be done! In essence this relational intention is to function towards everyone and everything and not merely significant others. Love is the most positive expression of personhood. Always, it creates an embracing and safe environment. The person related to in turn is helped in developing the ability to love, to practise compassion. Love as care is an attitude can be decided on and fostered. It is central to shaping a relationally meaningful life.

MOTIVATOR 2 *Authority/Responsibility*

Authority has become a maligned word with negative overtones. Without a structure of authority, however, anarchy soon rules. Authority and responsibility are two sides of the same coin. It is usually not essential to take responsibility for that over which I don't have authority. Vice versa, when the authority is mine, I must make sure to be responsible with it. In personhood, positive self-determination means using my inner freedom in an appropriate way. I must learn to live within relational boundaries that are beneficial to self and all. It prevents hurts and heartaches. Real personal freedom involves taking responsibility.

MOTIVATOR 3   *Unity/Integrity*

Unity in the context of personhood makes becoming an integrated personality possible. Being someone who seeks harmony rather than discord. Not at the expense of personally held value convictions though. Agreeing to disagree is always an option. But the relational intent must remain towards respect for the other and a desire to understand. Only someone of integrity can function in this manner. There must be an openness that engenders trust and a relational environment that is predictable. Consistency is a key. Positive, singular people are great to be with and foster inner strength in others. It is essential in making wellbeing possible.

TRINITARIAN RELATIONAL MODEL

The nature of human relating and its consequences can be explained in a simple model. The positive side is based on relational dynamics found in the Trinity. The negative represent how sin operates relationally as an opposite.

These dynamics are active automatically within every person. There is never a void. Deep-seated attitudes are derived from it. When the good isn't focused on, the bad will take control.

Adequate relating requires effort and understanding. The Trinitarian Relational Model can be of help in this. An outline of the three positive principles now follow.

MOTIVATOR 1 Love/Care

1. *Fundamental Orientation*
Love
I will think favourably of others and be merciful.

2. *Primary Expression*
Care
I will provide for and watch over.

3. *Technique*
Kindness
I will be patient and forgiving.

4. *Relational Interaction*
Understanding
I will be humble and remember my vulnerability.

5. *Basic Attitude*
Other-centeredness
I have empathy and desire to be of help.

6. *Existential Reality*
Personal Development
I am committed to your identity formation.

7. *Primary Outcome*
Compassion
I will encourage you to care for others as you
yourself wish to be cared for.

MOTIVATOR 2   Authority/Responsibility

1. *Fundamental Orientation*
Authority
I will work towards the wellbeing of others and myself.

2. *Primary Expression*
Responsibility
I will respond to the needs of others.

3. *Technique*
Discipline
I will expect right application and restraint.

4. *Relational Interaction*
Enabling
I will encourage maturity.

5. *Basic Attitude*
Dependability
I will see matters through.

6. *Existential Reality*
Opportunity
It will encourage self-control.

7. *Primary Outcome*
Freedom
I will show you the way of personal liberty within the boundaries of wisdom.

MOTIVATOR 3   Unity/Integrity

1. *Fundamental Orientation*
Unity
I will seek harmony where no ethical and moral principles are at stake.

2. *Primary Expression*
Integrity
I will practise what I preach.

3. *Technique*
Consistency
I will not be unpredictable in attitude and behaviour.

4. *Relational Interaction*
Appreciation
I will show you respect.

5. *Basic Attitude*
Honesty
I will practise openness.

6. *Existential Reality*
Support
I seek to travel roads together.

7. *Primary Outcome*
Wholeness
I will help you in finding an integrated personality.

All is well with the Positive

The three primary outcomes of positive relating are a true enablement. Anyone consistently exposed to it is a fortunate and empowered person. Positive relating can become a habit that is integrated into personhood. Remembering to care, to be responsible and to show integrity, is possible even in difficult times. Mistakes will be made, but these are now understood for what they are. They don't remain hidden under a cloak of ignorance. It makes improvement possible.

Easy Reference Questions

The key questions to ask about positive relating are:

1. Is my thinking affirmative?
2. Am I willing to care?
3. Do I have a role to play?
4. Am I acting responsibly?
5. Am I showing integrity?
6. How about respect?

Beware of the negative

Positive relating has its opposition. It will activate when unchecked. In relating it is essential to concentrate on the positive for it nullifies the negative. That is best possible when negative is well understood. The three primary dynamics of negative relating are called Demoralisers.

DEMORALISER 1   *Dictatorship/Oppression*

The opposite of love is not hate. Rather, it is not caring. This attitude, when aggressive, results in dictatorship. Someone may well become oppressive in relating under the illusion that they are doing it 'for the best,' out of care. But caring in a way that makes people feel beleaguered, is not the care of love. Love liberates, even when a message may be an instruction or a reprimand. Excessive exposure to dictatorial relating, however disguised, will result in anger with the recipient. Best be careful and ask others whether they find you oppressive at times. Evaluate that honestly.

DEMORALISER 2   *Desertion/Neglect*

It is easy to walk away from a relational responsibility that is bothersome. To avoid involvement. Such neglect may come in subtle guises and be insufficiently noticed. I may fool myself in thinking that my responses matter little. But the person exposed to this disinterest will feel it acutely. Relational neglect is common and people learn to adept to it. When, however, someone is confronted continually with an ingrained attitude of relational desertion by significant others, anarchy will raise its ugly head. 'If you don't care, why should I?' is the powerless cry. Personal identity then has been weakened into an indiscriminate lashing out.

DEMORALISER 3 *Disharmony/Manipulation*
Manipulation is the third of the relational negatives. It refuses to help others towards empowerment and prefers to undermine. Manipulation infiltrates a person's identity structures seeking to take control. 'I will not let you make up your mind freely. You will feel beholden to my request.' It is subtle psychological warfare and often goes undetected. Most people do not even realise it when they are manipulative or being manipulated. It seems all so innocuous. The most effective mental response to manipulation is: 'I'm now being manipulated. I won't buy into it and will make up my own mind.' I can then make up my mind how to act. I may yet oblige but on my own terms. Long-term manipulation disintegrates the identity of the exposed person.

The three negative principles are outlined in the model as follows.

DEMORALISER 1   Dictatorship/Oppression

1. *Fundamental Orientation*
Dictatorship
I will have my way with little regard for others.

2. *Primary Expression*
Oppression
I am the enforcer of issues.

3. *Technique*
Rule
My demands will be met.

4. *Relational Interaction*
Compliance
I do not accept objections.

5. *Basic Attitude*
Dominance
You will succumb.

6. *Existential Reality*
Confinement
I can overpower you.

7. *Primary Outcome*
Rebellion
Your anger does not concern me.

DEMORALISER 2   Desertion/Neglect

1. *Fundamental Orientation*
Desertion
I refuse being responsible.

2. *Primary Expression*
Neglect
I can turn my back on you.

3. *Technique*
License
I leave you to your choices.

4. *Relational Interaction*
Being left at bay
I will not protect you.

5. *Basic Attitude*
Irresponsibility
I do not value you.

6. *Existential Reality*
Abandonment
I will not be found.

7. *Primary Outcome*
Anarchy
Destructiveness is not my worry.

DEMORALISER 3 Disharmony/Manipulation

1. *Fundamental Orientation*
Disharmony
I do not seek companionship.

2. *Primary Expression*
Manipulation
I will emotionally misuse you.

3. *Technique*
Lure
I will draw you in underhandedly.

4. *Relational Interaction*
Appeasement
I will set you to my personal advantage.

5. *Basic Attitude*
Coercion
I will pressure and persuade you.

6. *Existential Reality*
Blackmail
I will exploit your emotions and fears.

7. *Primary Outcome*
Weakness
Your vulnerability and disintegration do not concern me.

How to work the model

The simplest way is to remember the six previously mentioned easy reference questions. Make that a habit and relating will be okay. Also, become familiar with the Primary Outcome of each dynamic for it motivates towards the positive. Consider each dynamic in detail preferably more than once to gain a good understanding of what is involved and why. The terms used should make this well possible. In doing so, I must evaluate what the habitual nature of my relating might be like. Ask those close to me as well and make behavioural changes. That challenge will pay off handsomely.

Examples of such an exercise for two dynamics now follow. The other four are to be tackled in like manner. Preferably with pen in hand to jolt my memory later. Nothing worthwhile is life is ever easy. It's all a matter of how much I value success in a given area.

Love/Care

The Fundamental Orientation of Love is an attitude that bestows favour rather than being critical. I will presume the best in people. I am not unaware of someone's deficiencies, but decides to be merciful. Unless shunned I will not step away from a person in disappointment. Instead, I seek to Care, which is the Primary Expression and the active side of a Love motivation. Caring can be costly both emotionally and economically. My charity may be exploited. The demands for care must be judged on their merit. Going the extra mile need not necessarily become two.

Love/Care as a Technique is marked by Kindness. It prefers to be friendly and patient. I will forgive and not always hold to account, though at times that may be necessary. Kindness is not a doormat, but projects a Relational Interaction that shows Understanding. People who understand well remember their own vulnerability and will be humble. They are good people to be with.

These qualities are expressed due to a Basic Attitude of Other-centeredness. My intention is to be of help and to show empathy. The environment on offer is one of support. The Existential Reality thus created engenders Personal Development. As someone who understands the relational dynamic of Love/Care well, I will always commit to a person's positive identity formation.

As a Love/Care person I will be compassionate. It enables others to become likewise. Compassion is the Primary Outcome of Love as a motivation. Exposure to compassion encourages compassion. I must care for others as I wish to be cared for. This ability develops from having been exposed to healthy relational dynamics. If I decide to Care my self-worth increases accordingly.

The negative dynamic selected for this exercise involves Manipulation, a subtle and destructive relational fault with dire consequences.

Disharmony/Manipulation

Manipulation demoralises. It is the Primary Expression of a Fundamental Orientation that sows Disharmony. Manipulation uses psychological pressure to advantage. Being subtle and destructive it is, at its worst, a form of emotional abuse. Manipulation undermines rather than empowers. The Technique used is to Lure a person into my purposes underhandedly. The Relational Interaction demands an Appeasement with the agenda of the manipulator. It can be innocuous but is psychologically harmful none the less.

The Basic Attitude behind manipulation is Coercion. I apply emotional pressure to persuade someone to act as I desire. It creates an Existential Reality that infers, 'I will not let you make up your mind for yourself.' It is a form of Blackmail for it exploits feelings and fears. This may not be obvious and properly recognised. Not even by the perpetrator. But the relational message will have its effects. Habitual Disharmony/Manipulation infiltrates a person's identity structures. It seeks to take control. The Primary Outcome of such relating is Weakness. A person consistently exposed to manipulation, while possibly depending on the manipulator's care, will become overly vulnerable. A disintegration of identity is possible.

Possibe demoralisation when confronted with negative relating highlights the importance of being informed about the relational and to detect its dynamics.

Relational Self-talk

Relationality is the most important dynamic in human life. That included relating to my own person. When relating to myself, self-talk is a key. Is my talk positive or negative? Which dynamics are in play? I must question how my mental messages correspond with the Trinitarian Relational Model.

There is no good reason that insists on talking myself down. Nor to subscribe to the thought of, 'if nobody else cares about me, why should I?' Neither is it helpful to be untruthful to myself. Rather, I must owe up to the reality of my self-perceptions. I must be honest while aiming for the positive. Call a spade a spade where necessary but care about my psycho-spiritual wellbeing. Be responsible without aiming for perfection. Good enough will do fine. I am inclined to give myself a break, but not foolishly so.

The Spiritual

Relating is a dynamic of my spirit. Like me, everyone may call on the 'Great Spirit' – compassionate and good – for help. It will empower Christian and non-Christian alike. The Christian knows this help as the Lord Jesus.

Thank you for reading this book

For more please see the final pages.

Best wishes,

Michael

Books by Michael J Spyker
Available at agapedeum.com

Trilogy

Meeting Emma

A journey of discovery in which Emma becomes familiar with the many idea of Christian Spirituality through the ages. It helps her towards the person she would like to be. This book has assisted many in coming to love the vast wealth of the Christians spiritual tradition.

The Primacy of Love

Jake hears about his father's ideas on God's Love from Baz while travelling the Simpson Desert. Their talks include the significance of eternal and universal love, and the relational. The story has been called a significant theological feat.

The Language of Love

Emma and Jake fall in love. JH introduces them to the real meaning of Eros well beyond merely sex. They learn about being a Friend of Jesus and the language of love. Emma and Jake set off camping in the outback in search of JH. They work out what it means to live intimately together.

Novels

Julian's Windows

A musician and a teacher of children with intellectual ability fall in love. He lost his wife. She questions her vocation as a religious sister. Country life in Victoria restores his soul. A holiday in Australia from Liverpool decides her future. The ideas of Lady Julian of Norwich are an integral part of this love story in a most natural way. Great fun and informative.

Shalomat

Jacq and Ahmed, 16 years old, are on the run through Australia on a quest with mystical dimensions. It draws them together. All seems lost but isn't quite. Young people and adults enjoy this adventure. It is partly a comment on the one-sidedness of modern society and uses ideas of spirituality and philosophy. Will there be a sequel, an appreciative reader asked?

Treatise

Science and Spirit

Science exists by the creativity of God. But where to find God within physics? Where in society, in which God has become irrelevant? An informed answer best includes knowledge of history, science, philosophy, theology and religion. Plus ideas about a way forward. A read of significance to enjoy.

Christian Living

Drawings and Reflections

52 short reflections and 16 drawings that lift the spirit. A brief story that sows an idea. A picture to enjoy. It is not so easy to stay focused in a busy world. A little help always comes in handy. There is nothing religious about this book apart from keeping Jesus in mind and living vibrantly.

REFERENECES

[1] 1 John 4:8

[2] Col. 1:15-17

[3] Kelsey, MT 1981, *Caring*, Paulist Press, NY p. 7

[4] Not to be confused with charity, which a dictionary may describe as universal love.

[5] Gen.1:31

[6] Mark 12:30-31

[7] 1 John 5:3

[8] 1 John 4: 8

[9] Col. 3:12-14

[10] Phil. 2:7

[11] Griffiths, B 1995, *Pathways to the Supreme*, HarperCollins Publishers, London, pp. 104-105

[12] Rolle, R 1972, *The Fire of Love*, Penguin Books, London, p. 93

[13] Ruusbroec, J 1985, *John Ruusbroec- The Spiritual Espousals and on the works*, Paulist Press, NY p. 247

[14] Ruusbroec, J 1985, *John Ruusbroec- The Spiritual Espousals and on the works*, Paulist Press, NY p. 24

[15] Ibid, p. 145 I have taken the liberty to replace the words man and men in the quote with person and people

[16] *The Collected Works of St. John of the Cross*, 1991, ICS Publications, Washington DC p.642

[17] Ibid, p. 642

[18] Norwich, J 1978, *Julian of Norwich – Showings*, Paulist Press, NY p. 148

[19] Ibid, p. 305

[20] 1 Cor. 13:12

[21] Mat. 5:48 Jesus encourages his disciples towards the perfection of God in love, which must be a reference to how God is perfect.

REFERENECES

[22] Horgan, J 1996, *The End of Science*, Little, Brown and Company, London p. 67

[23] Ibid, p. 57-58

[24] 1 Peter 1:15

[25] Merkle, JC (ed.) 1985, *Abraham Joshua Heschel – exploring his life and thought*, MacMillan Publishing Company, NY p.p. 67-68

[26] Ibid, p. 71

[27] Whitehead, AN 1929, *Process and Reality: an essay in cosmology*, Free Press p. 23

[28] Pannenberg, W 1990, *Metaphysics and the Idea of God*, W.B. Eerdmans, Grand Rapids p. 118

[29] Pannenberg, W 1990, *Metaphysics and the Idea of God*, W.B. Eerdmans, Grand Rapids p. 118

[30] Oliver, HH 1981, *A Relational Metaphysic*, Martinus Nijhoff Publishers, The Hague p.95

[31] Ibid. p.p. 154-155

[32] Ibid. p.156

[33] Ibid. p.170

[34] Phil. 2:6-7

[35] Luke 2:22-35

[36] Luke 2:41-52

[37] 2 Cor. 12:1-4

[38] Heb. 4:15

[39] Mat .3:13-17

[40] When his disciples asked Jesus to show them the Father he responded by stating: 'Who has seen me has seen the Father. ... Do you not believe that I am in the Father and the Father in me?' John 14:9-10

[41] 2 Cor. 5:21

[42] Gen. 3:1-7

[43] Mk 6:34

[44] John 5:36

REFERENECES

[45] Mark 9:23

[46] John 8:31-46

[47] John 2:15

[48] John 8:58

[49] John 21:25

[50] John 5:17

[51] Matthew 5 ff

[52] 1 Cor. 13:5

[53] 1 Cor. 13:4

[54] Gen. 3:5

[55] 2 Phil. 2:7

[56] Heb. 4:15

[57] 2 Cor. 5:21

[58] Norwich, J 1978, *Julian of Norwich – Showings*, Paulist Press, NY p. 213

[59] 1 Cor. 15:14

[60] John 20:19

[61] John 21:4

[62] John 3:7

[63] Mat. 13:18-30

[64] Rom. 8:21

[65] 2Cor. 5:17

[66] Rom. 7:21-25

[67] Rom. 6:14

[68] Rom. 5:17

[69] Rom. 8:11

[70] Tanner, L 2003, *Crowded Lives*, Pluto Press Australia, Melbourne p. 111

[71] Grenz, S 2001, *The Social God and the Relational Self*, WJK Press, Kentucky p. 76

[72] Etymonline.com

[73] Stendahl, K 1976, *Paul Among Jews and Gentiles*, Fortress Press, Philadelphia p. 85

REFERENECES

[74] Grenz, SJ 2001, *The Social God and the Relational Self*, WJK Press, Kentucky p. 196.

[75] Brunner, E 1939, *Man in Revolt*, Lutterworth Press, London p. 106

[76] Gen. 2:7

[77] John 20:22

[78] 1 Cor. 15:20-28

[79] John 16:12-16

[80] John 20:21

[81] John 17

[82] Grenz, S J 2001, *The Social God and the Relational Self*, WJK Press, Kentucky p.94

[83] Prof. Dr J. Court

[84] *The Collected Works of St. John of the Cross*, 1991, ICS Publications, Washington DC p.58

[85] 2 Cor. 5:10

[86] 1 Cor. 2:10-15

[87] Mat. 6:9-15

[88] Mat. 7:21-23

[89] John 5:25-29

[90] Rom. 2:14-16

[91] Mat. 25:31-46

[92] Sweeney, J M 2017, *Inventing Hell*, ACTA Publications, Chicago

[93] 1 Cor. 2:9